Puffin Books
Editor: Kaye Webb
Things to Do

Bored on a rainy afternoon? Fed up with playing the same old games? Perhaps you're on holiday in the country or in a big city and don't know what to do? Then be a magician; keep an indoor zoo or start a bonsai tree. Make your own guitar, design a glove-puppet or make an orange-peel belt. Try phoning a friend on your own home-made telephone or start a treasure hunt, practise brass rubbing or grow a 'squirting cucumber'!

Everything in this book has been thoroughly tried and tested by the author and her family. You need not buy expensive materials and, though the ideas are simple and practical, they are great fun to carry out.

Why not start now? There's no time to lose!

Hazel Evans

Things to Do

Puffin Books

Puffin Books
Penguin Books Ltd,
Harmondsworth, Middlesex, England
Penguin Books,
625 Madison Avenue, New York, New York 10022, U.S.A.
Penguin Books Australia Ltd,
Ringwood, Victoria, Australia
Penguin Books Canada Ltd,
41 Steelcase Road West, Markham, Ontario, Canada
Penguin Books (N.Z.) Ltd,
182–190 Wairau Road, Auckland 10, New Zealand

First published by Ebury Press 1974
Published in Puffin Books 1976

Made and printed in Great Britain by
Richard Clay (The Chaucer Press) Ltd,
Bungay, Suffolk
Set in Linotype Baskerville

In memory of my father, who never quite knew what to give me to do, and with thanks to Chris and Liz for their help . . . and for Nick in Bahrein, one of the children for whom this book is written.

Contents

Introduction 9

Things to Do in the Country 11

When You're Living in Town 27

For Rainy Days 41

Making Music 57

Home-made Magic 70

Kitchen Cunning 80

Ideas for Your Party 93

Pencil and Paper 107

On the Move 118

Odds and Ends 126

Things to Do in the Garden 141

When You're Ill 154

Where to Find What 162

Introduction

When I was young, I never seemed to have anything to do, mainly because my sister was away ill in hospital and every Saturday and Sunday my parents went to see her, but I wasn't allowed in. Left by myself rather a lot, I did the most extraordinary things: I conscripted an army of children with dustbin lids for shields and marched down the High Street, I opened a café in my front garden and sold – or, rather tried to sell – dog biscuits and ice cubes as teas. I ground up chalk on a cheese grater and tried to sell it in match boxes as face powder (I must have had a strong commercial streak in me) and I wrote books at the age of eight in which fantastic things happened to the heroines.

What disappointed me most of all during those years were the Things to Do annuals that people gave me, because the things they suggested either involved buying something very expensive, or something poisonous that the chemist would not sell you, or using a razor blade, tins and sharp knives. Or else the models they told you to make were so complicated that I would burst into tears from sheer frustration, trying to construct them.

In this book I've tried to make everything in it possible to do with the help of things you might find around the house. I've tried not to cost you too much money in materials, and my own children have a stern watch on my wilder flights of fancy. Even the most stupid grown-up should be able to follow the instructions, because I did – I have done everything that I have written about to make sure it works.

Things to Do in the Country

The country is full of exciting things to do. If you've
lived there, you know very well how to spend your
time, I'm sure, but if you've just moved out from the
city, or gone there for a holiday, you might not know
where to begin. Most things that can be done in the
country work perfectly well in open spaces and parks
too, so children who live in the suburbs or even in
towns will find some useful things in this chapter.
Indeed, most of the games can be played in your own
back garden.

Making a tent

You don't need to have a ready-made tent for camping, in fact it's a great deal more fun to make your
own if you can find a large enough piece of material
to use. A sheet or a blanket will do, provided you're
not trying to keep the rain out. Whatever you end
up with mustn't be too light or the wind will catch
it and you will have a job to make it stay put. There
are two ways of using a sheet as a tent. The easiest,
quickest one is to make an imitation ridge tent – if
you have two trees growing conveniently near by,
or a tree and a post that are near each other. First
fold your sheet in half, short sides together, and
measure that length. Now tie some tough cord or
rope from one tree to the other at that height, less
12 inches, like a washing line. Now simply hang
your sheet over the cord, spread out the sides and
then weigh them down at the bottom edge with
stones, leaving some sheet free at one end to tuck
in as tent flaps.

The other version, which looks a bit like a bell tent, only needs one post or tree. Tie your piece of cord as high as you possibly can, then stretch it at an angle of 45° – that's halfway between upright and ground level – and fasten it there (a meat skewer or a forked stick makes a good anchor). Fold the sheet over the line as before and fasten the top securely by untwisting the cord and nipping a piece of the centre edge in between.

Common sense about camping

If you've got a sleeping bag, use one. That pioneering stuff is all very well but it can be very cold at night and damp too, and sleeping bags are usually waterproof. Otherwise, if you can lay your hands on some, a heap of dried bracken makes a marvellous mattress. A pillow is something you needn't pack. Just place your shoes toe to toe at the top of your head, so they form a nice head-sized dip, then fold your clothes and lay them over this. It's surprisingly comfortable. Don't forget to take some waterproof plasters with you; I hope you won't have any minor accidents but if you are walking any distance your shoes can give you blisters on your toes, in places where they've never hurt before.

When you're ready to pitch your camp, see which way the wind is blowing first. How? It's easy. Just look at the movement the bushes and trees make and which direction they bend. If you pitch your tent with its back to the wind, it will be much warmer and more comfortable that way. Don't park yourself in a deep dip or at the bottom of a hill – the ground will almost certainly be wet. And *do* ask the farmer's permission first if you're pitching tent on private land. It could be that that bright green 'grass' you are about to walk over isn't grass at all, but a growing crop – or it could be that he lets his herd of pedigree bulls out into that field in the early hours of the morning! Either way, it is essential to ask him.

Building a fire

The easiest way to make a camp fire is to cheat a little and take along some dry newspaper, a fire-lighter or some charcoal. To make a fire safely, never never lay it on grass – lift off an area of turf first and lay your fire on bare soil, ring it with large stones to make sure it can't spread. Then, when you finish, you can use the piece of turf to smother any embers that are left smouldering. If you find some good-sized logs, place them in a circle, ends together in the centre like the spokes of a bike then, as they burn, you simply push the ends inwards with your foot and there's no fear that they will topple over. Take some food that's easy to cook – chipolata sausages and small potatoes in their jackets for instance, with forks to toast bread on. Always make sure before you leave the camp that the fire is completely out or, if it's still smouldering, that there is nothing near by to catch light.

Pocket sundial

Even if you haven't got a watch, you can still tell the time when you're camping with a home-made pocket sundial (see diagrams on p. 14). You need a stiff piece of card about 15 cm square (the side of a cereal packet will do). Now draw the largest circle you can get on the card, using a plate. Then mark your circle into 12 equal spaces round the outside, like a clock – start off with the halves and quarters, then go on from there. Draw in the numbers of the hours from 1–12. Find the centre of the circle with a compass or crossed rulers, and draw a line from there to the edge at 12 o'clock. Cut another piece of cardboard in a wedge shape with one side the exact length of the line you've drawn, and stand it at right

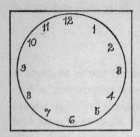

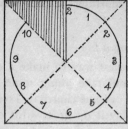

Telling the time from a home-made pocket sundial.

Using a watch as a compass.

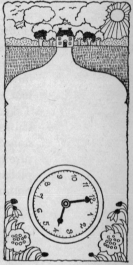

angles on this line so that the pointed end is in the centre, the wide part at the edge. Fix it in place with adhesive tape.

To tell the time, put your sundial on a flat surface, make sure the marker is perfectly upright, and turn the card so that 6 o'clock faces north. Look at the shadow the marker casts on the dial – the number it falls on is the hour. Remember that this is Greenwich Mean Time, so if our clocks have been put back or forward you'll have to allow for it.

Using a watch as a compass

If you do own a watch, or can borrow one, it can be used quite easily as a makeshift compass (see diagram opposite), so that you can tell which way you are heading. It sounds rather difficult but don't be put off – once you've got the hang of it, it is very quick and easy to do, and surprisingly right in its results. You need the help of the sun, so you must choose a bright day for your experiment, but it is difficult to do with the sun right overhead, so try not to attempt it at midday.

Take off your wrist-watch and lay it on a flat surface (the ground will do splendidly for this) and turn it so that the hour hand points exactly in the direction of the sun. Let's say that the time is 4 o'clock, so swivel your watch round so that the figure 4 points to the sun (now you can see why we can't very well do it at midday with the sun over our heads instead of being in a pointable direction). Count how many minutes there are between the hour (in this case 4 and 12), choosing the shortest way round the dial. If it is 4 o'clock, then there are 20 minutes between 12 and 4. Divide them in the middle and the answer is 10 – 2 o'clock exactly on the dial. And that point is where south is. North is exactly the opposite way, 8 o'clock on your dial. If you are doing this before 12 noon, then you work in the same way, but the result is the opposite way round – 2 o'clock would then be pointing north and not south. Now try it for yourself – it's fun to do.

Getting your bearings

There are other ways of working out which way is a southerly direction, using your eyes alone to help you instead of a compass. How? By looking closely at the things around you in the countryside. Look at the trees, first of all, particularly at the edge of a wood. Their bark will be lighter and drier on the southern side, while the north side of the tree will appear darker and damper, and may even have moss growing on it. Spiders, who like the warmth, usually weave their webs on the southern side of bushes, and whippy, spindly trees will tend to bend towards the south and the sun, while a stone or rock will only grow moss on its northern side unless, of course, there is water dripping on to it. The north side of a hill will be more green than the southerly side, but things growing on it will take longer to come into flower. You can see this quite clearly if you walk across a ridge of hills like the downs in Sussex, for instance.

One or other of these country signs on its own will not necessarily tell you which way south is in a completely foolproof way but piece one or two of the clues together, and if they all fit, you can be almost 100 per cent safe in guessing your direction.

Laying a trail

Following a trail set by somebody else can be a lot of fun if there are two sets of you, the hunters and the hunted. You divide into two groups, draw lots as to who should lay the trail and who should follow it, then give the trail-makers a good hour's start to lay their tracks and get well out of the way, cross-country. The most exciting trails are those that you make up for yourself (see diagrams on pp. 162–3), little signs and clues that others have to be sharp to spot. Tramps have used secret signs for years to tell each other which houses are hospitable to visit and which are not, where they are likely to be harassed by police or park attendants, which places are good to sleep in for the night. And there's no reason why you should not make up your own secret code too.

If you live in a chalky area, then you have plenty of natural material around to chalk secret signs on farm gates or rocks, or you could bend branches or tie knots in long grass to mark your way. At one time paper-chases were in fashion as a form of country tracking, but we are all so conscious now of the mess that pieces of paper make, scattered all over the countryside, that it is nicer to use something else instead. A trail of small pebbles is not too difficult to follow, but you will need several trail-makers to carry them – they'd be far too heavy a load for one person. We've had a very successful day's tracking using rose-petals to lay the trail. At the right time of year in any garden that has a respectable-sized rose bed, there is no problem in picking up good hand-fuls of fallen petals. They are obligingly light to carry and their colour shows up well, scattered across a field.

Space-age semaphore

Another way of communicating in the countryside that you might like to try is signalling across a long-ish distance by using semaphore. It's an easy alpha-bet to learn, and, anyway, you can carry a copy of the code with you (see over at top). Flags are the usual choice for sending semaphore messages, but you could equally well make yourself a space-age semaphore kit using large discs or squares covered with aluminium foil – the kind your mother keeps in the kitchen – stuck into a notch in the stick (see diagrams over at bottom). The silver discs have the advantage that they don't flap about, so the exact position of your arms is not difficult to see. On a sunny day they will catch the light and shine, almost as if you were using a lamp for your signal sending.

A 1 B 2 C 3 D 4 E 5 F 6 G 7 H 8 I 9

O P Q R S T U

Work out this message from the semaphore code above (for solution see p. 163). Note that when not in use, the flag is held pointing to the feet, as in the letters A, B, D, E.

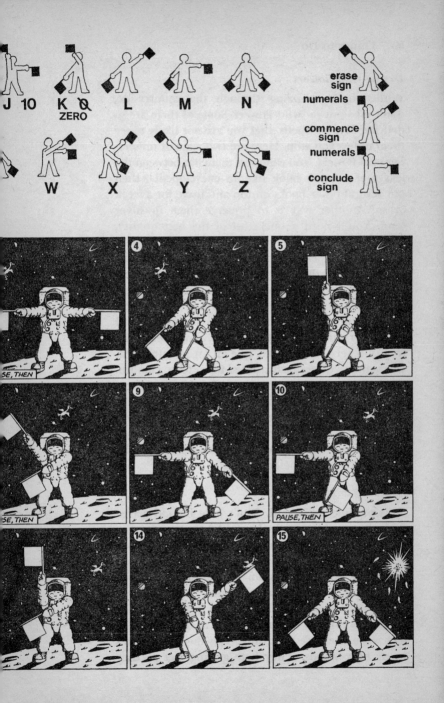

Drying wild flowers

While you're whizzing through the countryside, don't miss out on wild flowers. Some of them are so delicate, like harebells, that you are not likely to see them unless you stop. Here are two ways of preserving wild flowers. You can press them flat between the leaves of a heavy book like an encyclopedia, then put several other books on top and leave for a week or so. Another way is to preserve them in silver sand. You'll need a bucketful of the best quality. Take a deep dish or tray and line it first with a piece of blotting paper. Now sprinkle on a layer of the clean sand and then, very carefully, place the flowers on top arranged in the way you want them.

Now comes the tricky bit – sprinkle sand on top very carefully so you don't damage the petals, until the flowers are completely hidden. Then leave the tray in a very warm place, like an airing cupboard, where they will not be disturbed for at least a month. Then delicately shake off the sand until the flowers are uncovered. You'll find that they've kept their colour in a remarkable way and look as though they are still alive. They can now be mounted and framed and made into a picture. Leaves can also be dried by the same method.

Tracking wild life

This pastime takes skill. Don't hide behind a tree to look at wild animals – you'll have to move to see them. Instead flatten yourself in front, and keep very still. Always move slowly and stay down-wind, as the big game hunters do. That is, make sure the wind blows *towards* you, otherwise the animal will detect you by your smell. The best time to look for animals is early in the morning, or at the end of the day when they are returning. You might see foxes in or near woods. They hate getting wet so they won't cross a stream unless they have to. Stoats and weasels like woods, too. The stoat is so greedy he not only tracks down rabbits and big birds, but takes eggs, frogs or worms, too; he often kills just for fun. The weasel prefers mice and small birds for supper. Rabbits' warrens are easily found, particularly in sand, while hares live above ground in small hollows in the grass or bracken. Night time is the best time to look for hedgehogs, by the edge of a wood or by a stream – that's when they come out for insects. For a start, see how many creatures you can make out in the drawing on pp. 24–5.

Keeping ants

Talking of insects, you can have a lot of fun watching ants. They're found in colonies under a stone or in the ground. Ants will eat sugar but they particularly like tiny insects like greenfly which they 'milk' by stroking them. After we'd killed the greenfly on some flowers, we once watched an ant come to milk them, circling round them puzzled, waving its antennae, wondering why they did not move. It's easy to scoop up a colony of ants and keep them for a while in a glass-roofed home so you can watch them at work (see sketch on p. 22). First you will need two pieces of glass approximately 30 cm square. Place one sheet of glass on the ground, roll out a giant sausage of putty or Plasticine and curl it into a big circle on the glass. Now press a plastic drinking straw across the putty in one corner of the glass, and a piece of string at the other. Shovel your ants and some earth into the centre of the sausage, then quickly put the second piece of glass on top, so the ants are the meat in a sandwich. Put out a saucer of water and dip the end of the string into it like a wick. Push the end of the straw into a tilted box of honey or sugar, and cover the box with a piece of stocking so that the air can get in but the ants can't get out. You'll find that the ants will suck the water up the string when they want to drink, and will use the straw as a passage-way to get to the honey.

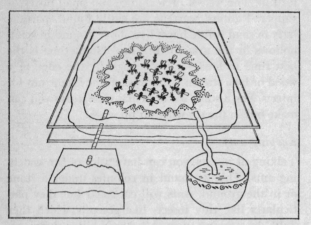

Watching an ant colony at work.

How to find fossils

There are all sorts of secret signs in the countryside that can tell you, if you do a little detective work, a great deal about what it was like not just hundreds, but thousands of years ago – that is, if you know how to look for them. What kind of soil have you got in your area? If it's limestone, shale or chalk, then the chances are you might be lucky and be able to find signs of life that existed millions of years ago. I'm talking about fossils, bones of tiny animals or shellfish that have been turned into stone, or have crumbled away leaving a perfect imprint of themselves in a piece of rock. There are even plant fossils, too, but they are more rare.

Where should you look for them? In stone quarries or on the base of cliffs, in newly ploughed fields where nothing has been cultivated before – ask the farmer first, though, in case he's seeded it. And, easiest of all – and that's where town children come in, too – where there are any road works going on or new housing estates being built. Huge earth-moving machines scoop and cut right through solid chalk and bring up lots of fossils. You'll also even find them lying on the surface of ground that's been worn away by heavy rain which washed away the earth around them. What do they look like? Rather like marks and shapes scratched in chalk – see some in your local museum.

History in glass

But fossils are not the only thing to look for; pre-historic weapons like arrow heads can be found if you are sharp enough to recognize them. Going forward now in time, settlers like the Romans and even medieval monks seem to have left a lot of litter. The Romans, for instance, liked oysters very much, and I know a field which has a lot of oyster shells lying on the surface. Little pieces of pottery can tell a story, too, and pieces of glass. Strangely enough, early glass was very thin, it didn't get thick until medieval times. If you think you've found something really exciting, go to your local museum and they'll be able to tell you all about it. Where to look for these things? A good map will help you if you read it carefully, for prehistoric forts, encampments and tumuli – ancient burial grounds – are all marked on it, so are things like stone quarries and pits, for you to explore.

Bird-watching

Looking at birds is a fascinating way of spending an afternoon. Some of them are so comical that they beat TV, any time. The best time for bird-watching is in the spring when they are choosing their mates and building nests, or again in the autumn, when many of them are getting ready for a move to some-

where warm. You can even be lazy and coax the birds to come to you in your garden, if you put out scraps of bacon rind, crumbs and nuts.

The beak and feet of a bird give a clue to its habits.

It's interesting to see which birds go for which kinds of food. Birds that like nuts or seeds always have short, sharp beaks like the chaffinch. Birds that like worms have long, strong beaks so they can grasp them and tug them out of the ground – they'll go for the bacon – just watch a blackbird or thrush. Insect-catching birds like the swallow have finer

beaks which can open wide and snap like pincers on their prey. Rooks, starlings and other hungry feeders have beaks like pickaxes so they can attack fruit and dig grubs out of the earth, while ducks have useful scoop-like beaks for burrowing in mud.

Feet can tell you a lot about birds too (see drawings above). Thrushes, sparrows, robins, birds that perch a lot, have three claws in front and one at the back to balance them on wobbly poles or fences. Other birds who need to be quick to catch insects

have smaller feet with all the claws in the same
direction to give less wind resistance. Everyone
knows that ducks have webbed feet, but so do lots of
other birds that paddle in the water.

Really keen bird-watchers build hideouts from
twigs and branches and creepers so they can't be
seen. That way you can see the whole cycle of nesting, hatching and the feeding of the baby birds and
their attempts to fly. When you are in a hide, as it
is called, you must keep your body very still and
your eyes and ears active. Make a note of the birds
that you see, or, better still, photograph them if you
can borrow a camera, then you can look them up
later on.

When You're Living in Town

A lot of people who live in towns just don't *use* them properly. Instead they sit indoors and mope about all the things they could do if they lived in the country without realizing what is happening on their doorstep, for a town is a living, growing thing too. How much do you know about your town's history, for instance? There are all sorts of interesting reasons why a settlement of people has grown up in a particular place – and that goes even for the most modern towns which don't seem to have any past at all. Sometimes it is because it's the exact spot where two valleys meet, a crossing place for communications. Sometimes it is because the river was shallow at that point in early days, a very important thing before bridges were built. Or your town may be on the top of a hill because it had a natural defence that way against invaders. Do *you* know why your town is there? It's surprising how much water plays a part in a town's history. Many places in the north of England for instance have grown up around spinning and weaving factories because the water in that area was just right for processing wool while Burton-on-Trent has a special kind of water that makes good beer – that's why there are so many breweries there.

Making a 'time map'

If you're interested in history, you could make yourself a time map of the place where you live, perhaps the very road. It takes quite a lot of skill but it's well worth doing. Supposing, for instance, you live in a place that has a lot of old buildings as well as a lot of new ones, see if your local library has a street plan of the town as it used to be in Victorian times. If they haven't, then your Town Hall or your local council offices should have one. Make a careful copy of your town centre as it was a century ago, then draw a map of it as it is today on tracing paper on top – then see how many buildings are still standing. Next try to predict what your town will look like in the year 2000 – you should be able to find out from your local paper, your library or the council all about plans for new shopping centres, new houses and motorways, all the things that alter the look of a place on the map, for they have to be planned years ahead.

As I sit writing this I can see a new road being built in the distance that is going to alter the town where I live a great deal. It will change it from a place whose narrow streets are choked up with big lorries, vans and cars all trying to get through, to something like the sleepy place that it used to be in the eighteenth century. This is happening to a lot of towns now, and changing people's lives at the same time – is this going to happen to you? You could easily find out.

Brass rubbing

Making brass rubbings of things of interest is one way of recording a town's history, but a lot of people are put off the idea of doing this because they think, quite wrongly, that you can only make brass rubbings of brass plates and monuments in churches, and if they haven't got a particularly interesting church in their town there doesn't seem much point in trying. But you can make a brass rubbing of anything where the lettering or the design stands out well from the metal or stone it is made from.

Take man-hole covers, for instance; you find them

in pavements everywhere and some of them are very old, and have really interesting, curly decorations on them, particularly the Victorian ones. Look out, too, for things like fire marks, left over from the days when there wasn't a fire service as such, but lots of different fire brigades employed by insurance companies, all with their special marks. Then there are often interesting brass plates on doors and other decorations on buildings. Or, on a smaller scale, horse brasses make attractive rubbings.

Making an impression

How do you make a brass rubbing? It's easy. Try this way to start. Take a 10p piece, put a sheet of plain paper over it, and scribble all over that with a pencil so that the image comes through. Got the idea? Well, you're doing that on a larger scale with a special crayon, or piece of heel-ball, to make your brass rubbing. You can buy special kits now in art shops for this purpose (see *Where to Find What*) but you can do just as well with a roll of lining paper from a decorating shop (several of you could buy one roll between you), a large very soft pencil, heel-ball crayon or wax crayons. If you want to be adventurous, though, you don't have to stick to white paper. You can buy dark paper instead and go over it with a heel-ball crayon in gold or silver, or a whole pack of crayons or chalks rubbed in bands over, say, a man-hole cover, to give it a rainbow look. (If you use chalk or charcoal for this job, you must spray if afterwards with a special fixative or it will smudge.)

All you need apart from that is a blunt, whippy sort of knife to scrape dirt and grease off the subject of your rubbing – you won't need to do that in a church, of course, but you might in a dirty, busy street. If you're taking a rubbing in a church, or on the wall of someone's building, ask for permission

This rubbing of a 15th-century floor brass in Blickling parish church, Norfolk, commemorates Roger Calthorpe, his wife and their 16 children. (The central section of the Latin inscription has been left out for reasons of space.)

before you start – I've never heard of anyone being refused. Lay your paper on top of the object. If it is on a wall, fix it in place with sticky tape, if it's on the pavement, weigh it down at the corners; either way make sure it won't move about as you work on it.

Now systematically rub over the paper with the crayon or heel-ball until the image appears. If the relief on the decoration is very clear indeed you could use a fabric crayon on thin material to make a brass rubbing that you could turn into a wall hanging or cushion afterwards. Otherwise most people pin brass rubbings on the wall as they would posters. (See example opposite.)

Exploring by bus

There are all sorts of games you can play in a town without having to go to a recreation ground and kick a ball around, all sorts of things to explore, too. But first of all you've got to know your way around, and if you don't know your town very well, this is where buses come in. A lot of children get taken to school by car now, or walk there, and miss a lot of fun riding on a bus. You can buy special Rover tickets that will allow you to ride around for as long as you like in any one day for one price (on p. 94 I tell you how you can make a party out of this). There are others that let you go out into the country and back again, so ask your local bus station about it. It's the cheapest and easiest way to get to know a big town, especially if you're a newcomer, and plotting your way from one point to another, with the help of a bus timetable, can be quite a complicated and interesting business. You could use your special bus ticket to plan a Town Treasure Hunt. For this you need a number of players for the best effect. Make out a list of items to be collected – a discarded 5p bus ticket, a feather, a brown button, a travel agent's brochure – anything and everything you can think of that could be found, but not bought in a shop. Everyone sets out at the same time with his list and the first one home with all the treasure complete is the winner.

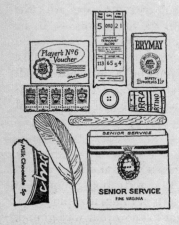

LIST OF OBJECTS TO FIND IN TOWN

1 A Cigarette Coupon
2 A Bus Ticket
3 A Match Box
4 Green Shield Stamps
5 A Button
6 A Cork
7 An Ice Lolly Stick
8 A Chocolate Paper
9 A Feather
10 A Cigarette Packet

Here are some of the things that players might be asked to find in a Town Treasure Hunt.

Two town games

Another similar sort of game that makes a town into a playground is Window Shopping. One person goes out in the morning and makes a list of some of the most unusual things they have seen in shop windows – red carpeting with white spots on it, a picture of a shipwreck, some straw hats from Jamaica – it could be anything. They then hand a list of the items to the rest of the team who have to set out and track them down – and write in which shop window they found them. Some of the best shops for this are antique ones which have a whole collection of un-usual things placed next to each other, anything from Victorian teapots to stuffed birds. To make it even harder you can write the items down in conundrum form like 'I have eyes but cannot see' (a potato).

If your town is the kind that has lots of small twisty streets, then Spies is another game that goes down well. One person is chosen to be the spy and is given a secret letter to leave in a secret place (that could be anywhere – a hollow tree stump in the park, a loose brick in a wall, under the doormat on someone's front step). He is also allowed to take with him some disguise in a carrier bag so he can change his identity somewhere along the route – a change of coat, for instance from the colour of the one he set out in, a pullover or a hat. You make your own rules as to whether or not the spy is allowed to board a bus or two, and you send him or her out, waiting until the spy has disappeared from sight, count 10, then follow. It's surprising how easy it is to lose someone, even in quite a small town – try it for yourselves and see!

Be an antique dealer

What else can you do in a town? I know several older children who are interested in antiques and they look out for little pieces of pottery and small ornaments, which they find going cheaply in junk shops. They clean them up, repair them, then often sell them again to another shopkeeper and make some pocket money that way. It is quite easy to become an expert on some very small specialized thing – clay pipes, for instance, or snuff-boxes – by reading up about it and looking at specimens in museums and very soon you find you know more about them than the person who is selling them to you. If you've a chance to lay your hands on fossils, flints, pieces of Roman pottery – which you might well be able to do if they are excavating for building in your town – then you can start your own museum. Who knows, you might find something interesting enough for your town's museum to take from you.

Helping other people

There are a lot of things you can do in a town to help other people. You could go shopping for someone who is old, and can't get out very much – your Citizens' Advice Bureau or local w.r.v.s. would know who they are. This way you could be rewarded by some interesting stories from them of what life was like in the town when they were children (I met a fascinating old lady once that way). There are lots of other ways of helping, too – Oxfam, Shelter and other organizations like that are always grateful for unwanted things you could collect from your neighbours and give to them.

A miniature zoo

What else? Well, you could have your own zoo. Where? Right on your own window-sill if it's large enough, or on a table that is pushed up near the window. Or perhaps outside, if you've got a small garden or a yard. For there's no end of insects, reptiles and other things you can keep in a town for no cost at all – moths and butterflies, beetles and bugs, spiders, frogs, tadpoles and woodlice. All you need for your basic equipment are some large jam or pickle jars, a cardboard box or two, perhaps a tin or a wooden box, and some plastic bags, sticky tape and pieces of netting or perforated zinc. Cardboard boxes are fine to start with for some insects, but you can't use them out-of-doors and they can't be cleaned very well. But if you line them with tinfoil, the kind that your mother uses in the kitchen, and then with newspaper, you can use them for a while as you can lift out the linings and replace them. Better still, of course, are boxes made from wood or from tin, for they can become permanent homes. Plastic boxes are good, too, for creatures like frogs or beetles that like a dampish place to live in, for water tends to collect on the sides and drip down again.

There are a lot of places where you can buy unusual exotic insects and reptiles for pets – we list some of them in *Where to Find What*. You can, for instance, buy specimens from a butterfly farm. But these things can cost a lot of money and some of these pets need special living conditions, so it's best to start on the home-grown variety that you can find free.

Rearing butterflies and moths

Let's start off with butterflies and moths, both of which you'll find in town gardens or in a park or on allotments. They start laying their eggs in May to September, according to what kind they are, so all through summer you should be able to find either eggs or caterpillars on the underside of leaves.

Look carefully underneath the leaves of plants like cabbages, nettles and chickweed and you should be lucky – though some eggs are so small that you almost need a magnifying glass to spot them. Pick the whole leaf, don't try to handle either a caterpillar or eggs direct, in case you damage them, and put it in a cardboard box, making sure that you know what plant it is, so that you can collect more leaves to serve as insect food. Transfer your collection to a stout cardboard box or, better still, a wooden one, with a sheet of clear plastic across the top with ventilation holes punched in it. (Remember that caterpillars can climb, so don't make the holes too large.) Put some earth in the bottom and a few pieces of leaf or branch inside to make it feel at home. Butterfly caterpillars hook themselves on to a piece of twig when the time comes for them to shed their skins, while moth caterpillars burrow into the earth, so if you're not sure which you've got, put in both so as to be sure they've got what they need.

Your caterpillar will feed happily on its leaves until the time comes for its fantastic transformation scene to begin. It will shed its skin, leaving a curious mummified-looking shape which just hangs there, apparently doing nothing. Then gradually the butterfly comes out, with its wings not quite formed at first. After half an hour or so the wings have appeared and, after about another hour, they have hardened enough for it to fly. Now the time has come for it to be released.

The two kinds of caterpillars you're most likely to find in a town are the greeny-yellowy ones of the large white butterfly, which you'll find on cabbages, and the woolly bear caterpillar of the garden tiger moth (it's easily recognized because it's covered with long woolly hairs) which eats from ragged-leaved plants like chickweed. It's a sad fact that although you might be lucky and find a painted lady or a red admiral, some of our most beautiful and colourful butterflies have become so rare now that they are almost non-existent, killed off by chemicals and air pollution. Be careful, won't you, that the box in which you keep your caterpillars and, later on the pupae, as they are called at transformation stage, is not left in hot sunlight or too near a radiator, or the unfortunate insects may cook. It doesn't hurt to give their box a spray from time to time with a fine mist of water – perhaps your parents have a special sprayer that they use in a greenhouse, for instance, for the pupae must not get too dry.

Lively beetles

These creatures make lively and sometimes rather comical town pets. You'll find them in dark, damp corners of old houses, under rotten pieces of tree, scurrying under dried leaves. Once again, like the caterpillar, their grubs are found where their food is, so these are the surroundings you have to imitate if you are going to keep them in a box.

Beetle grubs behave just like caterpillars and

Butterflies and
moths go through
many interesting
stages.
Right: garden
tiger moth.
Far right: red
admiral.
Below, centre:
butterflies.

become pupae before turning into their eventual beetle shape. Beetles are a lot more sensitive than most people realize; there is one called the bombardier, for instance, that squirts a small amount of poison gas around itself when it is frightened by something. Several of them make noises, too – one of the funniest ones is the click beetle which has a habit of falling over on its back, then jumping up like a jumping bean, making clicking noises at the same time; it's called a wireworm at grub stage – something all gardeners hate.

Snails and frog-spawn

Snails are something else that you could keep in a town zoo. They curl up inside their shells to sleep all winter, of course, but in summer they can be interesting to observe and they've the advantage that they're very easy to catch! A snail likes a miniature garden to live in, so give it some growing plants, the ones you found around it when you caught it. Snails are best kept in a disused aquarium, so you can watch them slither up the glass sides, but they are equally happy in a box.

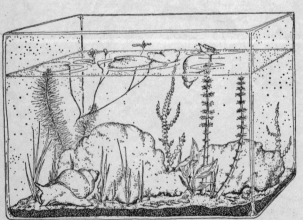

You can watch water snails at work if you fill an aquarium with pond water and grow some plants; frog spawn will thrive here too.

There are so many books around on keeping fish that I won't go into it here. But don't forget that frog-spawn, collected in the spring, is a good thing to keep on your window-sill zoo, and in the first stages all you need to house it is a large jam jar. (Better still, though, put it in a proper aquarium with pond water, some weed and other things you may collect at the same time like water snails.) When the time comes that the tadpoles are turning into frogs then it's best to let them loose at the pond where you found the spawn. But you could keep a couple of frogs as pets if you have a large glass tank to put them in. Line the bottom with some earth and some stones and give them a dish of water. Unless your tank is very deep, you'll have to put a ventilated lid on it and find food for the frogs – they like insects, with pieces of worm and slugs as a special treat.

More for your window-sill zoo

Another insect-eater that is hard to catch but easy to keep is the lizard. Grass snakes could be kept in a window-sill zoo, too, but there's something of a problem there, because *their* favourite diet is a frog or two, and it doesn't seem right, somehow, to feed one of your guests to another. Crickets and grass-hoppers can be kept on a window-sill, too – you can catch them sometimes in a park by shaking the branch of a low bush or tree or searching carefully through long grass. Grasshoppers, as their name suggests, live mainly on grass, but crickets are more house-trained – they like a few biscuit crumbs, some cooked mashed potato, even cabbage scraps.

Something else that is very small and would fit on the most minute window-sill and is very easy to feed is the silver-fish – not a fish at all but that quick-silver, darting thing you see sometimes in damp places in old houses. They move with amazing speed, so you've got to be quick to catch them but once caught they will live happily in a cardboard box with a piece of perforated plastic on top. They like any food so long as it's starchy – flour, powdered rice, even cake crumbs.

If you don't suffer from creepy-crawly-itis, as I do, house spiders make interesting pets – that is if you are cold-blooded enough to be able to catch live insects and flies for them. But even writing about spiders makes me shudder, so I'll leave you to find out about them on your own!

For Rainy Days

Wet weather can be a chance to do all sorts of things you haven't time to settle down to ordinarily. For instance, have you ever thought about making your own magazine? It's as good a way as any I know of spending your time on one of those long weekends when it rains and rains and you're stuck indoors. As long as there are enough of you each to do something and make the magazine really lively, you can turn out something different that makes truly interesting reading and, most important of all, is extremely worth-while doing.

Planning your magazine

Just as a real-life magazine editor has to work out what he or she is going to put on the pages, it pays for you to plan, first of all, what features you are going to put in. The liveliest magazine would be a mixture of local affairs, readers' letters (to get a few arguments going), perhaps a short story if there is somebody who is willing to write one, a poem, some cartoons – the things you can put in it are limitless – it all depends on what talent you have in hand.

'Printing' the copies

To do a magazine properly you should produce more than one copy. And that may seem difficult without a printing press. But if you buy or beg some carbon paper (try to get black rather than blue), use typing paper and press hard enough, you should be able to get out several copies at a time – I've just tried writing on typing paper with a rather blunt pencil and got six carbon copies out without any difficulty at all. I am assuming that you haven't got anyone to type it out for you – with a typewriter you could probably do more (if you have a typist, tell her to switch her machine on to 'stencil' – you won't get a top copy, but all the ones underneath will be much sharper and look as if they have been printed).

Providing the pictures

What are you going to do about illustrations? Drawings are easy enough, you just get the artist to press heavily on your top copy, but supposing you wanted to use a photograph, what could you do then? Two things, actually. If it is a good quality photo in another magazine, or an original one, it might pay you to have it photo-copied by machine. Get together all the photographs you want done in this way, arrange them all on one sheet on paper, glue them down, then take them to any firm that does photo-copying (there are often do-it-yourself ones in stationers' shops). For a few pence you'll be able to get as many copies as you need; they won't be particularly clear, but they'll be usable. If your photographs appear in a newspaper, there's an even easier way: rub some clear candle-wax over a smooth piece of paper, put the paper, wax-side-down on the newspaper picture, and rub the back of it as hard as you can with the bowl of a metal spoon. When you lift the paper you'll find that the photograph has been transferred on to the paper as a negative. Trim the edges of the paper round the picture, put it wax-side-down on to your magazine, run the spoon over the back again – and hey presto, your picture has been transferred. You need to do this same operation for each magazine copy, of course.

Appointing your staff

It's a good idea to appoint someone as art editor, so that when the contributions come in, he or she can arrange them in the best way on a page. If you haven't a typist to hand, then someone with the best handwriting will have to be the 'printer'. If you're doing several copies at a time, staple or pin the pages and carbons together at *all* corners, so that the under ones don't slip about while you are drawing or writing on the top. If you really want the magazine to look professional, it would be a good idea to splurge a few pence on buying a sheet or two of Letraset, or any other kind of instant transfer lettering for headlines and titles – otherwise you could buy a stencil set and use that for a neat look.

Making a chess set

What else can you do on a rainy day? It's frustrating if you're stuck indoors and you want to play cards, draughts, or chess and find you haven't got a set in the house. But there's nothing to stop you making your own in a matter of minutes. As long as you've got some stiffish card, it doesn't take long to make your own pack of cards – speed things up by making stencils of the diamond, heart, spade and club shapes – and you can really let your imagination run riot on the faces of the Kings, Queens and Jacks.

A chess board is easy enough to draw up in black and white – you need 64 squares altogether, by the way, 8 along each side of the big square. Chessmen can be made from anything – cardboard cut-outs stuck in pieces of sliced-up medicine bottle cork for bases, or more ambitious ones carved out of pieces of potato or moulded from modelling clay. The shapes you want, just to remind you, are the King, Queen, two rooks (usually shown as castles), two bishops, two knights (shown as horses' heads) and

eight pawns each. You can make a set of draughts
easily, too, either by painting one set of 12 coins
white and leaving another 12 as they are, or using
large buttons, or circles of cork, or our old friend
the potato again.

Snakes and ladders set

As long as you've got a die and some counters or
buttons, you could make your own splendid snakes
and ladders board with more violent snakes and
longer ladders than you get on bought ones. All
you have to do is to get a large piece of cardboard
or some very stiff paper, mark it up into rows, then
squares (it doesn't matter in the least how many
they go up to), mark them with numbers, starting at
the bottom and working across, then up – then draw
in your snakes and ladders all over the board.

Home-made skittles

Plastic bottles – the kind used for washing-up liquid
– are so useful to have for different kinds of things
that you should persuade your mother to let you
have them when she has finished with them. If you
do have a hoard, then you can use them for skittles
on a rainy day when you've nothing to do. Paint
them bright colours and if they have a tendency to
fall over by themselves, without being hit by a ball,
push a few dried peas or beans or beads through
their necks so that their weight at the bottom of
the bottle will keep it upright: there'll be more

Plastic bottles
can be painted to
make a set of
skittles; push a
handful of dried
peas through the
neck to make
them stand firmly.

things to do with plastic bottles in Chapter 4. Balloon tennis and paper football are two rather batty games for a rainy day – they both tend to make rather a lot of noise, and are not awfully kind to the furniture, so it's a good idea *not* to do them in the living-room, or near something fragile like a television set.

Balloon tennis and paper football

Balloon tennis is a very frustrating game (well, have *you* ever tried to hit a balloon really hard with the flat of your hand) and one that grown-ups tend to make asses of themselves playing, but I love it. You clear the room as much as you can. Put a line of chairs across the middle for a tennis 'net', placing each chair facing in alternate directions so each side has its share of chair seats as hazards. The idea is, quite simply, to hit the balloon on to the floor of your opponent's side of the room. If it lands on a chair, table or sideboard, that doesn't count. It can be quite an athletic game if you have to clamber all over the furniture to retrieve the balloon and it can be made into a much faster game if you use table-tennis bats instead of hands.

Paper football is even more noisy and needs still more room. In this case you would clear the centre of the room as well, but you need two goals, which could be between the legs of a table, in a corner, or under a chair – decide that beforehand. Your football is simply some crumpled newspaper crushed into a football shape and then sticky-taped into place. It doesn't last very long, of course, so you'll need a constant supply (come to think of it, there's no reason why you shouldn't use a balloon instead) and you can play the football with or without slippers on, depending on how rough the players are and how many hazards there are like chair legs and doorsteps to stub your toes on.

Shadowgraph shows

Here's an interesting kind of play you can do on a rainy day – it's particularly good if the weather is gloomy because the room is not too light and your shadows show up well. You've all, I'm sure, made animals' heads by interlocking your fingers and holding them up against the light so that their shadows are thrown on the wall. Well, shadowgraph shows are made the same way (see sketches below).

You'll need to rig up a theatre for your shadow show. The easiest way to do this is to stretch a sheet across the room as tightly as you can as a screen, then fix a light behind it. This can be either

How to make the shadows of various animals.

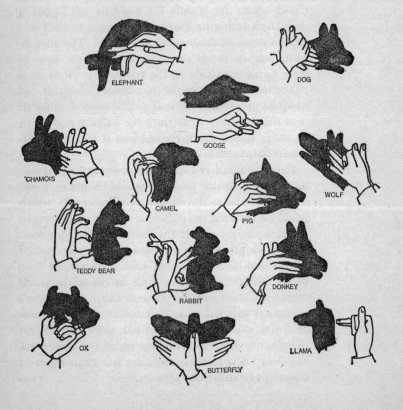

ELEPHANT

DOG

GOOSE

'CHAMOIS

CAMEL

WOLF

PIG

TEDDY BEAR

RABBIT

DONKEY

OX

BUTTERFLY

LLAMA

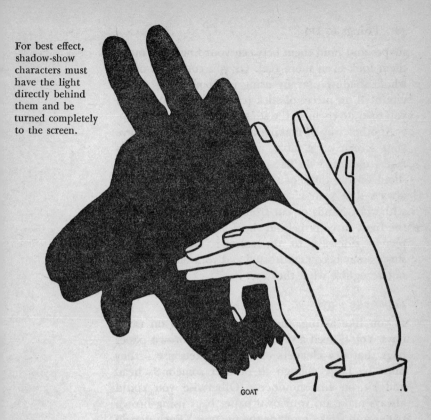

For best effect, shadow-show characters must have the light directly behind them and be turned completely to the screen.

GOAT

a powerful torch or, better still, a reading lamp put in such a way that it will 'throw' the shapes that you make on to the screen so that your audience can see them, but not you.

To make the simplest kind of animal, put out your hand and turn it sideways in front of you as if you were pointing the way. Stick your thumb up in the air to make an ear, bend up your first finger so that there is a hole between it, at the middle joint, and the finger below it, for an eye. Now drop your little finger so that a slit for the mouth appears. With the help of a few 'props' you can turn your hand into any number of characters. You can make cardboard cut-out hats, or cut-out animal head shapes and hold them between your fingers to make them look even more real. Or you could act out a whole shadow play by using cardboard silhouettes mounted on pieces of stick (crouch down low when you operate them so the stick can't be seen).

Another way of making a shadow show is to have your screen on a table, and have cardboard characters mounted on flat pieces of battening so they stand on the table of their own accord. Remember always that your characters, whether they're made with your hands or cut from cardboard, *must* have the light directly behind them and be turned completely sideways to the screen: otherwise their shapes may become distorted and your audience will not recognize what they are.

Paper-bag plays

If you like acting, these are good to do on rainy days. You'll need a supply of those big brown paper bags that dry cleaners or supermarkets use – they must be large enough to fit over someone's head and sit on his shoulders. (Otherwise you could always make up your own paper bags using brown paper and sticky tape for the purpose.) Each person becomes a character in the play, goes off with his paper bag and makes himself a suitable head and face out of it. You put the bag over your head, feel cautiously where your eyes are, and mark the places with chalk. You then mark your nose and mouth in the same way. Take the bag off, make a small hole for each eye, a slit for your mouth, and a hole to breathe through.

Then turn it into a face – paint on the kind of eyes you would really like to have, a huge red mouth, a tiny nose or whatever, or, if you are a character of some importance in the play, you will probably need a moustache, or a special face to go with it. Make paper-bag hair either by glueing on

All sorts of head-dresses can be made from large brown paper bags; a good way of spending a wet afternoon is to put on a paper-bag play.

curls made from strips of paper wound round a pencil or thick hunks of wool, or simply draw hair on the bag and paint it some suitable colour.

There could be paper-bag animals too, of course, and for these you may want to push and bend the bag around a bit to make ears, for instance. The plays you act can be as crazy or as serious as you like – I've found that folk tales like those rather horrific ones by the Brothers Grimm go down very well in paper-bag plays.

Doll with an old-fashioned look

If you've got one of those very cutie-pie modern dolls, and you wish you had an old-fashioned one instead, with the help of plaster you can actually change her face. Here's how: you'll need to buy some Gesso powder, a kind of plaster that can be got from art-supply shops. Gesso was used by Italian artists at one time to make frescoes (wall paintings) and it is a very fine type of plaster. Mix a little of the powder with some water until it is like a thick smooth cream, tie the doll's hair back away from her face, then paint the plaster mixture carefully all over it – if she has movable open-and-shut eyes, you will have to be careful to avoid them, but if her eyes are just painted on, you can coat them with plaster too. Let the first coat of Gesso dry – it doesn't take more than a few minutes – then take a look to see whether she needs a second coat of the mixture to cover her original features completely and give you a blank mask to work on.

As soon as the Gesso is completely dry – it will go very white – the doll is ready for her new face. You can fill in her features with water-colour, acrylic colour or felt-tipped pen, in fact any kind of paint that can be mixed with water. But I think that water-colour looks best for this because it has more delicate tones. The first thing to do is to get her skin colour right. Skin is not, as you might imagine, just a pale pink; there is some yellow and brown in it too. A professional painter will mix up colours like yellow ochre, white and cadmium red to get the right shade, and even add black for shadows – perhaps this will give you some ideas. You can, of course, buy flesh-coloured paint but it always looks too pink to me and I add a little yellow ochre to make it more realistic. You can even use real make-up on a Gesso-ed face. What happens if you don't like the look of it, and want to get it off again?

Just scrub at it hard with a brush and warm water and it will eventually come away. I've experimented, by the way, with Gesso on all kinds of plastic faces and found that it will stick to any of them from the hard, shiny ones to the soft, rubbery variety.

It's easy to make an attractive ring-holder using plaster of Paris to fill an old rubber glove. A useful door-stop could be made the same way by filling an old Wellington boot.

Ring-holders and door stops

Here's an interesting thing to do that is useful too. Mix plaster of Paris, fill an old household rubber glove with it (make sure it hasn't any holes in it – if there are, patch them with surgical tape) and hang the glove on a line to dry. Once the plaster is set you can peel the glove off and what have you got? A plaster hand that you can decorate and stand upright on your dressing-table to hold rings and bracelets; your mother might like one of these.

How to make a monster

Something for the boys now – what about making a few monsters? That's a good occupation for a rainy day. You'll need to collect lots of cartons and it's a help if you've got some silver spray paint, the kind that comes in an Aerosol can. Other things that are useful for monster-making are cotton reels, 'crown cork' bottle tops that rattle when strung together, cream cartons and a supply of wire and string. Decide whether you are going to make a space creature or some sort of mythical animal or insect – you'll certainly need silver paint for a space thing.

Start off with its body – and here that good old washing-up liquid plastic bottle comes in handy once more. As I suggested for the skittles, it's a good idea to pop one or two dried peas or beans in it before you use it – this time so that it makes a sinister rattle when you move it. Its head could be anything you fancy – a small square carton, a yoghurt pot turned upside down, a cigarette box – and you give it bulbous eyes by sticking on two bubbles from egg cartons. Its legs could be a mixture of crown cork tops and cotton reels, threaded on to string so they dangle. What makes the monster look really good is when it is sprayed or painted all one colour so that its different components, the bits and pieces attached to it, no longer look like bottle tops or cartons at all but part of one solid thing.

Thread all the pieces together with wire if you want your monster to stand solidly up, or with strong button thread if you want it to dangle. Dangling monsters should have a thread coming up through their heads so that you can attach a bar to it to dangle it from; that way you can make it 'walk' along beside you. A more complicated monster could have a battery hidden in its body linked up to two touch bulbs for eyes – cover the bulbs themselves with some pieces of clear plastic egg carton. You can make good antennae for it out of pipe cleaners. A very simple monster for a small child to make is a giant spider – simply stick some pipe cleaner legs into a big potato and spray the whole thing black – it looks really menacing. (See also drawing on p. 95.)

A bungalow for your dolls

Ever thought about making a dolls' house? It's surprisingly easy if you think in terms of bungalows rather than two-storey houses – then you can use cartons, boxes and odds and ends for the rooms and you don't have to worry about making stairs. It can be a super-modern house with a flat roof, too (no slopes to bother about), and it could have 'picture' windows made from clear plastic. The roof could be made into a roof garden with Plasticine earth and flowers.

Collect a supply of boxes that glued together make a network of rooms, then cut out doors and door-ways between them using a razor or sharp pen-knife. Wallpaper the walls with patterned paper you have made yourself, using paint or a felt-tipped pen for the pattern repeats. You can even wire the house up for electricity if you use small, simple batteries hidden in corners, one wired up to each light. What can you use for lamps? If the house is large enough, ping-pong balls with holes bored in them make splendid modern shades (hide your electric wiring, fix the wires in place by using surgical tape over them, then paint them to match the rest of the wall).

Making the furniture

Modern dolls'-house furniture is easy to make out of chunks of cardboard or polystyrene packing material glued together and covered with fabric (see p. 54). Don't forget pictures, either – tiny scraps or motifs cut out of magazine pictures look good and you can make picture frames out of matchsticks. What about books? That's simple – just cut up strips of fine corrugated card with an uneven top edge to give the impression of different-sized books, then paint each 'stripe' a different colour and each dent a dark shade for the shadow between them.

Once you start to 'think small', there's no end to what you can do – a handbag mirror becomes a king-sized mirrored wall in a bathroom, for instance.

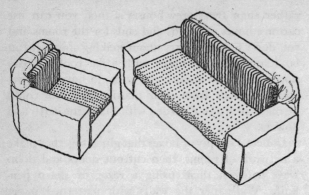

Polystyrene
packing material
can be covered
with fabric and
glued to make a
sofa and chair.

The bathroom and the kitchen are the two rooms
in a dolls' house where you may have to buy ready-
made fittings, but you can mould your own, if you
are clever enough, using self-hardening modelling
clay. Weave your own carpets or make them from
scraps of felt; bits of foam plastic decorated with
felt-tipped pen make marvellous upholstery and tiny
cushions.

Dolls'-house people

What about a family for your dolls' house – you
must make them yourself because they are such fun
to do. You'll need several packets of pipe cleaners
from the tobacconist for the job, a reel of surgical
tape from the chemist and some lengths of wool,
plus oddments of fabric for clothes. You'll need one
or two paper handkerchiefs, too, for moulding into
papier-mâché for their heads.

One and a half pipe cleaners used together make
the arms. Spread one pipe cleaner out fully, snip
the other one in half with wire cutters and bind
it with wool to the middle of the first one, so that
an equal amount overlaps at each end for the hands.
Bend the ends back into a u-bend about 15 mm long
and bind it with pink wool for the hands. Bind the
rest of the pipe cleaner with surgical tape to make

the arms a little fatter. Use two more pipe cleaners twisted loosely together and bound with plenty of tape for the body and neck, and then use the tape in a figure-of-eight to bind the arms across the body, just below the top. Make the legs by bending one pipe cleaner into a U shape, cutting a little off another cleaner and twisting it on to the first one leaving a gap at the ends, as you did for the arms; these are bound with wool and then bent into right angles for the feet. Fix the legs to the body at the U-bend with more surgical tape.

Make a head out of a well-soaked ball of papier-mâché (see p. 110) using paper handkerchiefs instead of newspaper for the job. Paint on a face, add some woollen hair and make a hole in the bottom of the head, poke the neck into place and fix it with a spot of glue.

Clothes for dolls of this size are best made with

Dolls' furniture can be made from wound and twisted pipe cleaners. The monkey has a cork body round which pipe cleaners have been wound; his eyes, mouth and shorts are made of felt.

the help of a glue like Copydex, rather than by trying to sew them, as it is difficult to make seams
without them looking clumsy.

Making Music

If John Lennon and Yoko Ono can make a best-selling record by banging a wardrobe door as an accompaniment, it just goes to show that you're not stuck with expensive instruments if you want to form your own pop group at home. For, as they showed with *Give Peace a Chance*, you're much more likely to come up with a new sound if you use unusual things rather than conventional ones to make music with.

Many of the pop groups are finding out that this is true. Take the Bonzo Dog Doo Dah Band – they played a length of hose pipe, a vacuum cleaner, and even a lavatory (don't ask me how!) in some of their recordings. The B.B.C.'s Radiophonic Workshop, too, positively pride themselves on collecting odd things like empty shampoo bottles to make the background music for some TV programmes.

Don't turn up your nose at those toy trumpets and things you get given at parties or in Christmas crackers, either. The Beatles used a cheap tin whistle as part of the backing for *Penny Lane*, and Ron Geesin, who writes film music, takes an ordinary toy trumpet for a lot of his effects. The recorder that so many of you learn now at school is also in fashion as a pop music instrument. The Move and Jethro Tull, too, both use the descant recorder for some of their records, and if you keep an ear open you'll hear it crop up on other people's records too. Bob Dylan and The Beatles have used mouth-organs to make music with. So really, when you think about it, everyone is likely to have some sort of musical instrument at home to form the start of a pop band.

Then when you add all the things around the house that can be used to make musical *sounds*, you're really getting somewhere. It's all up to your own enterprise. Bottles, tins, short pieces of plastic pipe, odds and ends from the kitchen and garage can all be used to make music.

You need two basic groups of things, instruments that will play a tune for you, the lead, and others that will give the rhythm and backing; and you've got to have at least one instrument from each group, even if you're being a one-man band, before you can start. The lead instruments in a pop group, folk, or jazz band are usually the guitar, the piano or the organ. Then they also use the recorder, the mouth-organ, trumpets, flutes and sometimes xylophones, too. The rhythm instruments are the drums, cymbals, the double bass and, for Latin American music, the maraccas.

Fortunately if we haven't got the instruments themselves, or we can't make them, we can very often imitate the sounds they produce by using something else – and that's what we're going to do, quite a lot of the time.

Getting a good sound

First get ready for action. You'll need a table to put your weirder instruments on, preferably *not* the one that your mother polishes daily with loving care. The kitchen or workshop table is your best choice, if you're allowed to take either of them over. You should also choose a rehearsal room, if you can, that doesn't have a lot of furniture or furnishings in it. Now let's take a look at some of the instruments we need.

Make your own Hill-Billy

You can make a Hill-Billy guitar quite easily if you have a little patience. If you have some pocket money to spend as well, you could turn out quite a professional instrument, for the strings, the tuning pegs, the bridge and even the neck and fretboard of a guitar can all be bought ready-made from a music shop. But, in that case, it would cost you anything up to £2.50, so we're talking about one made from scratch (see diagram below).

It's easy to make your own Hill-Billy guitar. You can either buy ready-made strings or make your own from piano wire.

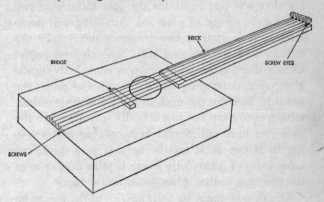

First, you need a wooden box. It can be any size, but the smaller it is, the more puny and high-pitched the notes will sound, so aim at finding something somewhere near guitar size. It needs to be made from smooth wood that is not too heavy, and it must not have a lot of cracks and holes in it (an orange-crate, for instance, would be useless). At a pinch you could use a smaller drawer from a disused dressing table; you can sometimes pick them up for next to nothing at junk shops. The box does not need to be shaped in any way, but it must be given a lid that fits tightly. The easiest way around this is to buy a piece of plywood (ask them to cut it to fit in the shop) but you could use hardboard if you wanted to.

Don't nail the lid on right away, divide it in half with a pencil line across, and cut a circle out of the middle of one of the halves. This is, quite simply, a hole for the sound to come out. It doesn't matter at all if your circle is not perfectly round, it can be as lop-sided as you like, provided the edges are smooth.

Next you'll need a piece of wood for the neck of the guitar, to carry the strings. If you can find some hardboard, mahogany for instance, so much the better, as it does not warp. I found a broken table leg that was just right for the job. Otherwise you can use an off-cut of plywood. Anything will do so long as it is at least two inches wide to take the strings, and flat on one side. Smooth and round off any sharp edges with a rasp or some heavy-grade glasspaper, depending on how rough and tough the wood is. Now fix the neck to the lid of your guitar, letting it overlap but not actually intrude on to the hole you have cut. Secure it by gluing and screwing it. If the wood for the neck is very thick, cut a piece out of it carefully where it joins the lid, as in the diagram, so that it lies flatter on the top.

You're now ready to nail the 'lid' of the guitar on to your sound-box, and it will begin to look a little more like a musical instrument, we hope. Next, you need a bridge to carry the strings. This is used to make sure that the strings don't actually touch the neck of the guitar unless you press them down on it to make a note. You'll need a strip of wood at least two inches wide (a piece of beading is fine) and it should be glued just below the hole you've cut for the sound to come out, and lined up with the stem so that the strings will pass over it.

At the bottom of the guitar, on the side edge, site six short screws to take the ends of the strings. Screw them in so they are just firm, but not too tight. At the top of the stem of your guitar, screw six screw eyes in a row, ready for the strings.

Stringing and tuning

Now you are ready to string your guitar. You'll need some piano wire, at least seven times the length of your finished guitar or, better still, a set of ready-made guitar strings from a music shop (they cost around 50p a set). Cut the wire into six equal lengths, or unwrap the strings. Tie each one round the bottom of a screw head at the base, and tighten up the screw, take up the slack and tie the other end round the screw eyes at the top. You tune your guitar by turning the screw eyes so that the string tightens or loosens. The tighter the string is, the higher the note.

How to tune your guitar? If you haven't got a piano handy you'll need a pitch pipe (you can get them from a music shop). This will give you the six basic guitar notes to line up with.

Facing your guitar, and reading from left to right, plucking each string in turn, you adjust the screw eyes to get the notes E, B (the one just below middle C) G, D, A and bass E.

Now press each string down in turn, working your finger down the neck of the guitar, identify the notes and mark out fret lines between them so you can find the same sound again. If you enjoy guitar playing, it will pay you to mark the frets more clearly by covering them with strips of fuse wire, wrapped round the neck. That way you can feel the position of the frets with your fingers instead of having to look down at them.

The three-chord trick

You'll find plenty of cheap teach-yourself guitar guides in the shops, but if you simply want to accompany yourself rather than play a tune, all you need to do is to learn the 'three-chord trick', as pop musicians call it. The three chords you need to know

are D major, A7 and G, and you'll find them written
out in *Where to Find What*.

With just one chord, D major, you can sing quite
a number of folk songs – *Barbara Allen, Swing Low,
Sweet Chariot* and *The Girl I Left Behind Me*,
for instance. With the two other chords in hand, you
can sing just about every folk song there is, and
make up your own pop songs as well.

Poor man's guitar

The most instant kind of stringed instrument you
can make is the poor man's guitar, which can't be
taken too seriously but is quick and easy to put together and play. You need a small cardboard box
for this, with a lid and a handful of rubber bands
of various sizes which will stretch over it. Following
the diagram, cut a hole, and a narrow slit in the
lid of the box. Now, out of the cardboard you have
cut away, make a 'bridge' for the guitar, a strip of
folded cardboard which fits tightly into the slot you
have cut and stands up in a ridge. Seal the lid of
the box down with sticky tape, then stretch six
rubber bands over it, choosing different sizes and
thicknesses, as far as possible, to vary the notes. The
smallest and most tightly stretched bands will produce the high notes for you, the thicker and less
stretched ones the lower notes.

To play your poor man's guitar, simply pluck at
the 'strings' with your fingers or, if it is very small
indeed, strum it with a matchstick.

Xylophones and bells

What else can you use to play the tunes for your
band? There are xylophones, bells and vibes, all of
which are used by pop groups and can be imitated
easily from things found around the house.

Eight milk bottles will give you the makings of a
good xylophone. Collect up some empty ones during

the week, or have a quick rally-round among your friends to make up the numbers. Range the bottles in a row on a table and tune them up to the eight notes of an octave by pouring water into them, little by little, the least in the bottle at one end, the most in the bottle at the other.

Eight milk bottles are all you need to make a xylophone; for a permanent collection, stock up some jam and pickle jars.

Compare the notes you get with those on a piano, recorder or pitch pipe to check them. When calculating the height of water you'll need in your milk bottles, remember that the more water you pour in, the lower the note is, the less you add, the higher. When you've got your levels right – and it may help to put a little colouring in the water so you can see it clearly – mark the spot and put the name of the note on it. Use sticky tape for this job, as the dairy doesn't take kindly to having its milk bottles painted.

To play your milk bottles, tap them with a spoon held rather loosely in your fingers. Once you get the hang of it you can turn out a tune quite fast. You can get even more effect from them, by the way, if you pick up each bottle as you play it, and blow across the top at the same time. This makes it sound as if the same note is being played by two instruments at once – a saxophone and a xylophone.

For more bell-like notes you can tie string carefully round the necks of the bottles and suspend

them on a rod slung between the backs of two chairs.
But make sure before you hoist them that you've
tied them properly or you'll have a lot of glass and
a lot of water to clear up.

Vibes

Large nails, suspended from a stick, make a pleasant
sound like vibes if you hit them with the side of a
knife blade, and they can be made to play a tune
if you can find several nails in various different sizes.

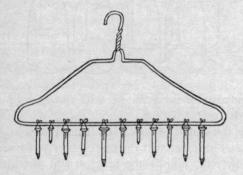

Assorted nails
tied to a wire
coat hanger make
a sound very like
vibes.

A piece of broomstick or a smoothed-down piece of
branch will do for the holder, or you could tie the
nails to the base of a metal coat hanger (see diagram
above) and hook it on to something. Suspend the
nails from the holder, tied up by their heads on a
short length of twine or button thread. Tie the other
end of the thread to the coat hanger or the stick,
spacing your nails about 2·5 cm apart so that they
do not touch each other when they swing. The nails
should not dangle more than 3–5 cm from the holder
or they will knot themselves into a tangle. This is a
good one for small children to play.

Home-made whistle

There's usually someone around with a recorder, but if you're stuck without any piped music, you can easily make your own penny whistle. Here's how you do it. Take a piece of plastic tubing, the rigid kind, or a cardboard tube (the sort used for posters and calendars). Alternatively, if you've nothing else, look for a nice, fat, straight piece of elder branch – you'll find elder bushes in lots of gardens, even in the suburbs – and scoop out all the soft pith.

Cover one end of the tube with a piece of Cellophane (a jam-pot cover is fine) and glue it in place or secure it tightly with an elastic band. Now punch eight holes at equal intervals along the tube – a skewer can be used for this job; it will even go through the plastic. Hold the pipe up to your lips, press them against the Cellophane and hum loudly into it, covering the holes one by one with your fingers to get different notes.

Making a musical saw

The musical saw, which used to be a star turn in the music halls, can be imitated quite easily without causing your father's displeasure. In other words you don't need to have a saw for this at all, you can use any flexible, whippy piece of metal. We found that one of those long flexible Meccano pieces worked excellently. This is what you do with it: stand the strip on end on the top of a table, bend it into a shape loosely like the figure 8, and saw up and down the side edge with the *blunt* edge of a knife. You'll find that by bending and straightening the piece of metal, and moving the knife you can produce a variety of wailing sounds, not unlike those of a baby crying – if there's a dog around the house he'll almost certainly start to howl at this one! With a lot of practice you can even play a tune, but it's quite fun, even without that.

Cymbals and drums

Now we'll move on to some things you can use for the rhythm and backing in your band. Cymbals are simple, just use saucepan lids, held by their handles and clashed together, or suspended by string from a stick and struck with a metal spoon.

Drums can be made in several ways, For loud, deep notes, try stretching a piece of plastic over a plastic bucket or a metal wastepaper basket (see sketch opposite). Hold the sheeting in place by a ring made from a length of elastic. You'll find that this job needs two people, one to hold the plastic in place while the other slips the elastic over it. The advantage of a drum of this kind is that it will stand up to quite a lot of drumming with real sticks, or with makeshift drumsticks – plastic shoe trees.

Smaller bongo drums are best made from an old cocoa tin with a piece of paper stretched over the top. It's annoying, but true, though, that there never *are* any empty cocoa tins around when you want them (at least, not in our house) so you may have to use something else instead. Cardboard tubes make good drums if you seal one end with stout paper, and those soft plastic bottles that hold washing-up liquid can have their tops cut off to form a drum base (volunteer to do lots of washing up, until you have succeeded in emptying one). Don't risk using any tin that has been opened by a tin opener unless the edges are absolutely smooth – a jagged edge would not only cut your fingers, but break the paper you stretch on top, too.

Making the drum top

Now for the drum top. Paper is fine for this, provided it is not too thick and unwieldy. Typing paper is quite good for the job, but the best kind of topping of all is Cellophane, so if you are making a small drum your mother may have a large jam-pot cover and a rubber band to spare which would be ideal. Whatever kind of paper you use, soak it for a second or two in a saucer of water, then spread it out carefully over the top of the 'drum', making sure it overlaps the sides all round. Then secure it quickly with an elastic band or piece of elastic before it dries and tautens up.

Plastic sheeting stretched over a bucket makes a good drum; use cocoa tins and paper for smaller drums.

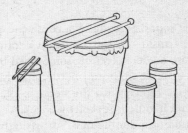

If you're using ordinary paper, rather than Cellophane, and have some dope of the kind used for making model planes, paint that on it to strengthen the surface. Play bongo drums by tapping them with your fingers, other drums by using strips of balsa wood as drumsticks, shoe-trees or plastic knitting needles. Remember not to go drum-crazy, if the top is made of paper, or you may bang too hard and go right through.

Maraccas and double bass

Maraccas are a must if you want a South American sound, and they're easily made from any container. A small tobacco tin, a cigar box, a cocoa tin are all fine if you put something that rattles inside them. Collect a few small buttons, some dried peas or some rice for this job. Experiment – you'll find different things make different sounds. And when you have made your mind up, don't forget to seal down the top with sticky tape, or the contents may fly out when you shake it.

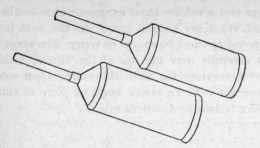

A plastic bottle, some dried beans and a stick are all you need to make a good maracca.

The best sound is made by a cocoa tin with some dried beans inside it, but the most exotic looking maraccas are made by feeding some dried beans into an empty washing-up liquid bottle, then ramming a piece of stick tightly into the neck, in place of the pourer, for a handle (see sketch above).

The sound of a double bass, surprisingly enough, can be got out of an ordinary wooden school ruler, this way. Place it flat on the edge of the table so that most of it projects over the side. Hold it in place with one hand, and twang the overhanging end with your thumb. You can alter the note by simply moving the ruler further on to, or off the table.

If there's a scrubbing board about (ask Grannie if she has got one, because they're rather out of date now, since washing machines came in) you can use it for a good rhythm backing for Folk or Hill-Billy music. You'll need several thimbles though (try Grannie again for these). Playing the scrubbing board, or wash-board as it is often called, is simple, you just hold it at an angle, and run your thimbled fingers briskly up and down to get a distinctive shuffling sound.

Get going

Now you've got your band together start off with a simple tune that everyone knows. Find out, before you allocate the instruments, which people can keep time, and which people can't. There's nothing more annoying than a player who is constantly off beat, so keep him or her away from the rhythm section.

If your lead instruments have difficulty with learning tunes, remember that the human voice is a very effective instrument, too – the Swingle Singers make a living out of singing Bach and Mozart. You can also disguise it well by singing down pieces of pipe, whistling or humming into something or even yodelling down the end of one of those long low vacuum cleaners to make a sound like bagpipes.

If someone has a tape recorder, you can have a lot of fun making your own recordings and seeing how many musical sounds you can get out of things around the house. And if the recorder has more than one track, with your parents' help you can be your own band – recording the backing first, then adding the tune with another instrument.

Home-made Magic

The most important thing to remember, if you want to be any good at all as a magician, is to *keep talking*, all the time. Keep your audience interested in you, your face, and what you are saying to them, and they're far less likely to notice if something goes wrong with a trick or see the mechanics of what you are doing. Next time there's a conjuror on television, watch him at work, and you'll find that he's talking away at you, all the time.

You don't have to have an expensive magician's kit to start up as an illusionist – though it's a nice thing to ask for for Christmas if you get really interested in doing tricks. Fortunately, there's all sorts of magic you can make, all sorts of tricks that you can try that really will make your audience believe you have some sort of supernatural power, all of them done with things you can find right now, around the house. Nothing more expensive, in fact, than a matchbox and a lump of sugar.

Magic matchbox

This trick can turn you into an instant magician very easily and it's an illusion which really does confuse your audience, especially grown-ups. All you need, as you've probably guessed, is a box of matches. Empty the box and put three matches on one side. Take them and tuck them away under the 'roof' of the outer covering of the empty matchbox while you carefully slide the tray part of the way back in place (you'll find you have to tilt it slightly downwards to get it in). The matches should end up so that their heads and part of their stalks are over-lapping on to the tray – but your audience won't see that, all they will see is an apparently empty match-box being waved in front of their noses. Now tell them that you are going to put three matches into

The matchbox trick is easy to do and very impressive.

the box by magic. Snap it shut completely, then open it again – and the hidden matches will have fallen into the tray (see diagrams below).

Magic messages

These aren't tricks in the strictest sense, but they're fun if you want to confuse someone at school, and pass on a secret message at the same time. But it needs patience and a sharp pencil to do these signs which can be seen, but are impossible to read unless you know how. You must print the message, not write it in script, and you make each letter very long (about two inches high is the right measure-ment) very thin, and very close together indeed, apart from the gaps between words. To make it easier to read afterwards, darken the top and bottom of each letter in the word so that it is thick and black.

The result is rather as if you had printed some-thing on a wide piece of elastic, then stretched it into an even taller shape, and it is just as distorted to look at – rather like a balloon with a message on it before you blow it up. You'll find that your mes-sage is impossible to read at all now, unless you know the secret formula which is this: tilt the paper until it is on a direct line with your vision – tip it this way and that until suddenly you'll find you can read it quite clearly. It's a matter of getting exactly the right angle. Anyone who isn't in the know will look down on it at right angles in the usual way, and not be able to make head or tail of it.

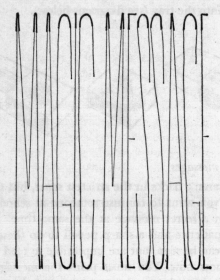

Messages should be written in tall thin capitals, very close together; the top and bottom of each letter should be darkened. To read them, the trick is to tilt the page away from you and down; you will be able to read the words easily.

Secret language

The best way to *speak* a magic message to someone is to use Pig Latin, a fake language that schoolboys have been using for years. You simply take the first letter of every word and put it at the end, then add -ay. *Oday ouyay eesay hatway Iay eanmay*? If you've managed to work that out, then you're well away, for it looks far more complicated written down than it is to speak. With practice you'll be able to rattle off a conversation with each other that leaves everyone else totally mystified – try it on a bus journey for instance and see the reaction of people around you!

The magic mark

A moderately complicated trick using water is the 'magic mark', one to do when there are several people around because you need two helpers, and of course an admiring audience. Your equipment is simple – a glass of water, a sugar cube and a very soft pencil – try to get a 3B if possible. Choose two people to help you, and tell them that you are going to make one of them pass a secret sign to the other one without either of them touching each other. This, we hope, will make them stare at you with disbelief. Ask one helper to stand on one side of you, and one on the other. Make a great fuss about their not touching or speaking to each other at all.

Now ask helper No. 1 to write a secret sign with the pencil on one side of the sugar cube you give him, making sure that helper No. 2 cannot see what he has written. While he is doing this you have to prepare yourself for your part in the trick. Say, in a casual way, that you are feeling thirsty and will have some water while you wait. When you take a sip from the glass, make sure that in doing so you spill some of the water down its side – one way of getting round this is to top it up afterwards, rather clumsily, with water from a jug. Next, make sure you rub your thumb against the wet glass, to dampen it as you put it back on the table. Another way of getting your thumb wet without raising the suspicions of the audience would be to dip your thumb in to 'see if the water is cold enough'.

Next, get helper No. 1 to hold the marked sugar cube towards the audience, then say 'I'm going to put the sugar in the water now' and, as you do so, pick it up so that its marked side presses against your damp thumb. This acts like a transfer, and puts the mark on to *you* as well as on the sugar. Now quickly drop the cube in the water, marked side up, and ask helper No. 1 to cover the top with

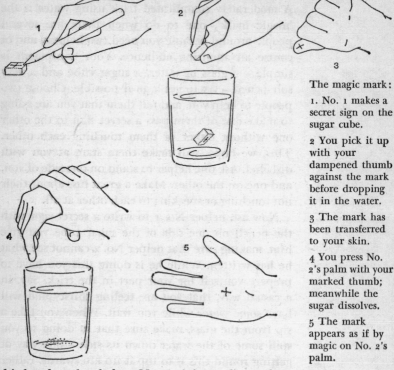

The magic mark:

1. No. 1 makes a secret sign on the sugar cube.

2 You pick it up with your dampened thumb against the mark before dropping it in the water.

3 The mark has been transferred to your skin.

4 You press No. 2's palm with your marked thumb; meanwhile the sugar dissolves.

5 The mark appears as if by magic on No. 2's palm.

his hand so that helper No. 2 can't see the mark on the sugar. As he does it, find fault with the way he puts his hand over the glass, say 'You must have three fingers sticking out,' or something like that, 'Look, I'll show you.'

Here's when you take helper No. 2's hand to demonstrate, and as you do so be sure to press lightly on his/her palm with your dampened thumb – then you'll have transferred the magic mark. Meanwhile the sugar will have been dissolving in the water, and the mark will have faded – show helper No. 1 this, and say 'It has been transferred by magic.' Get your second helper to turn his or her hand over and there, sure enough, is the mark (see diagram above).

Find the card

A very simple piece of magic that uses people from the audience is 'Find the Card' which is also a very good introduction to card tricks if you haven't done any before. You need to prepare your pack before-hand by putting them in a special order, so don't stand any nonsense from anyone who offers to shuffle the cards for you! The simplest thing to do is to put cards in their separate suits – all the Dia-monds from Ace up to King, in number order, for instance, followed by hearts, then Clubs. Or you could group all the Aces together, followed by all the Ones, and so on. The idea behind this order is that if any card is taken out of the pack and put back somewhere else, it is easy to see at a glance which one it is, since it is out of sequence.

Now ask several members of the audience to come up in turn, take a card from the pack, show it to the rest, then replace it in another position. When they do this they will, obviously, put it back out of sequence. All you have to do is take the pack in your hand, wave your magic wand over it, turn it face up, and start to count the cards out. As soon as you come to one out of sequence, hold it up to the audience and ask who it belonged to – they'll wonder how on earth you knew.

Undressing trick

If you can get an accomplice or an assistant, there are several good tricks you can do. You can start your act, too, in a slapstick way by saying to him 'I don't like that shirt you're wearing, I'm going to take it straight off you.' Then you get hold of his shirt by the scruff of the neck and pull it straight off him, apparently through his body and his jacket.

How's it done? Quite simply. You organize it all beforehand. Before the act starts you and your ac-complice shut yourselves away somewhere so he

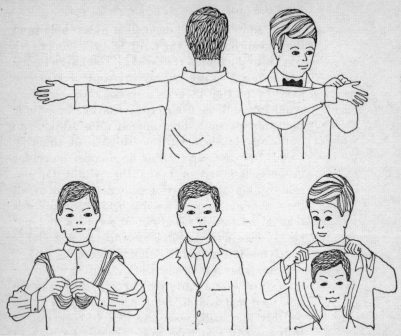

can take off his shirt and put it on again draped round his shoulders like a cloak. He does up the collar and the top buttons that show, then buttons the cuffs round his wrists *without* putting his arms into the sleeves – see what I mean? Finally, he puts his jacket on over the top, arranges the shirt so that it looks as though he is wearing it in the ordinary way. When you want to whisk it off, you simply undo his cuff buttons and shirt front while you are talking to him, then give a yank and it will come off (see drawings above).

Although your assistant appears to be wearing his shirt normally, it is really just draped round his shoulders and you can easily whisk it off.

Mesmerizing trick

One of the oldest magic jokes I know always goes down well at a party, but does tend to make rather a mess of the victim. For this you need two patterned plates that look the same, a candle, and something for mumbo-jumbo, like a handful of grains of rice. And, of course, you need a trusting, not too inquiring member of the audience for your victim. Say you are going to perform some magic ritual. Light the candle and place it on a table in front of your victim and hand him his plate (better make it a large one, by the way, so that he doesn't scorch his fingers). Get him to hold the plate in his left hand, over the candle. Take the other plate in your left hand (but don't of course, hold it over a candle) and scatter a few grains of rice on each plate.

What you do from then on is up to you – you've lots of scope for imagination in explaining to him and to the audience what a ritual is – you could say it is a beautifying ceremony (you'll see why in a minute) or that you are hoping for a message from the spirits. The whole object of the exercise is to get your victim to keep passing his plate over the flame of the candle – in that way depositing a lot of soot that he can't see on the underside. Give him a fixed stare so that he becomes so mesmerized by your dynamic personality that he doesn't realize what he is doing.

Go through a ritual of chanting, reminding him all the time to do exactly what you are doing, then, finally, rub your fingers under your (clean) plate, so that he does the same without realizing he is transferring soot on to himself. Finally pass your fingers over your face, either drawing in a mock moustache and eyebrows (if it is a beautifying process) or marking out some initials (if it is a message). By now the audience will be laughing, and it's time to produce a mirror and show your victim exactly what he has done to himself.

Magic mind reader

This is a trick that needs two people – you, the magician, go out of the room, while your assistant invites someone from the audience to choose any sentence in the book you are holding, and write it down with its page number on a piece of paper. He or she then goes back to her seat with the paper in her hand while another member of the audience takes the book outside to the 'magician' in the next room. After a suitable interval you come in, and amaze everyone by opening the book at the correct page, and reading the correct sentence.

How's it done? Easily. First choose a book which has a paper book jacket on it, then prepare it beforehand this way. Sellotape a sheet of paper to the front cover, with a sheet of carbon paper face downwards on top, then replace the book jacket on top in the usual way. When the member of the audience comes to write out the sentence and page number, make sure they use the front of the book to write on – that way the impression goes through the hidden carbon on to the paper beneath. You, the magician, then simply undo the book jacket, take off the carbon paper, make a note in your mind of the page and the sentence – then come in and do your stuff in front of the audience. Afterwards, the book can be safely passed round for the astounded audience to examine.

The smashed watch trick

Finally, on the subject of magic, here's a trick that really has a professional look about it, but does need some preparation. If anyone in the family breaks a watch, and the jeweller says he can't repair it, try to get it back to use for a trick. You could even ask a watch repairer, if you know one, if he has some broken watch parts to spare. With the sad remains of what was once a good watch you can easily do a trick that will terrify your family. You will also need a large paper bag, two handkerchiefs that look exactly the same – and a hammer.

Having got your audience assembled, ask your mother or father if you can borrow their watch for a moment. Wrap it carefully in one of the handkerchiefs, put it in the paper bag and say that you're leaving it there for the moment for safe keeping. Now explain that you are going, by magic, to turn the watch into two. You can take out of the paper bag the second handkerchief, not the first, in which you have already wrapped the broken pieces of watch. Put them on the table, and before anyone can realize what you are about to do, bang the handkerchief with a hammer – needless to say, you will check very carefully that you don't have your father's watch, but the pieces there, won't you? It is easy to tell which are which by feeling.

The hammering is guaranteed to bring horror to the grown-ups' faces and when you unwrap the handkerchief to show the broken pieces the effect will be riveting. Now say, 'Oh dear, it doesn't seem to have worked properly' or words to that effect. Wrap the pieces up in the handkerchief again and put it back in the bag. Now say, 'I'll just wave the hammer over it, this time, and see what happens.' Take the *other* handkerchief with the whole watch in it out, wave your hammer over it, then uncover the watch, intact.

The whole point of this trick is the surprise, so if you're able to get hold of some broken watch pieces, don't, whatever you do, tell anyone about it.

Kitchen Cunning

I'm going to start off with some cooking ideas, but there are a lot of things in this chapter that you don't *have* to do in the kitchen. In fact, you could do them anywhere you like in the house, but since they're inclined to be rather messy, I've included them here, because the kitchen is easily cleared up.

Cakes and sweets are not only fun to make but fun to eat afterwards as well, unlike some things like tapioca pudding, for instance (I used to call *that* frogs' eyes, I wonder if children still do?). The quickest cakes I know are the kind that are made with cornflakes or almost any kind of breakfast cereal.

Chocolate cookies

For these you'll need 200g of chocolate, a small piece of butter (just a knob) and some cereal. Break the chocolate up, put it in a small basin with the butter, then stand that in a saucepan with enough water in it to come halfway up the side, and heat it. The chocolate in the basin will slowly melt – but keep an eye on it because if the water boils over the top into the chocolate, then your cakes will be ruined.

Once the chocolate is nice and liquid, take the basin out of the saucepan, pick up a handful of cornflakes and stir them quickly in, add more cornflakes, stirring all the time, until the chocolate won't take any more. All you have to do then is to spoon dollops of the mixture into patty tins or on to a plate and leave them somewhere cool to set (a refrigerator is the best place).

You don't have to stick at just chocolate, you can make toffee cookies in just the same way.

Coconut ice

This is easy to do, and much cheaper than if you buy it in the shops. If you have some interesting cake colourings in the larder, you can turn it all sorts of lurid shades too – I once saw some blue coconut ice made that way. You need 200 g of desiccated coconut, 400 g of icing sugar and a tin of condensed milk. Sieve the icing sugar – you always have to do that before using it, as it very easily goes into lumps – then mix it together in a large bowl with the desiccated coconut (I say *large* bowl, because icing sugar tends to fly around in a kind of mist when you stir it).

Now add the condensed milk, little by little, working it well into the sugar and the coconut, and add the colouring, too, at this stage if you are using any. Keep adding the milk and pounding the mixture until it is a stiff ball in the bottom of the basin (you'll probably find you need about 5 or 6 tablespoonfuls of milk in all). Now turn your coconut ice on to a plain hard surface – glass, plastic or marble are fine, wood is not so good as the mixture seems to cling to it. Roll it out into a slab with a rolling pin or an empty, clean milk bottle and trim the edges (what do you do with the trimmings? eat them, of course!). Dust it with icing sugar, by shaking the empty packet over it (there's always some left inside), then leave it somewhere cool for an hour or two to set.

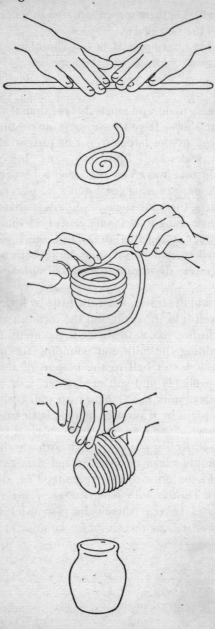

One way of
making a pot:
roll it into a
sausage, coil it
into a circle for
the base, then
build up the sides
by rolling the
snake round on
itself; the ridges
can be smoothed
out afterwards.

Pots from your garden clay

Cooking isn't the only thing you can do in the kitchen – as I said before, it's a good place to do all sorts of messy jobs, such as modelling in clay. Most people enjoy making pots, but have you ever thought about doing what they had to do, hundreds of years ago, and using earth from your own garden to make clay pots? It's perfectly possible if you happen to live in a part of the country that has a clay soil – and that goes for a lot of us. You can recognize clay easily enough. It's the kind of earth that goes as hard as iron, and cracks on the surface when it hasn't rained for a long time, is sticky and heavy and clings to your boots when it's wet.

Find out whether you've got clay in your garden; if you have you can dig some up, bring it into the kitchen and use it for making things. Dig up half a bucketful of soil, digging as deep as you can for it, then cover it with water for an hour or two to soften it up if it is at all dry. Now comes the really messy part which is best done out-of-doors: it must be sieved to get rid of any small stones, weeds – even beetles and worms – that may have got into it. For this you should use the kind of sieve that is specially designed for gardens or for sifting ash from a fire, but if you haven't one like that to hand, you could use a colander instead (remember to wash it well afterwards).

After the earth has been sifted into a fresh bucket, and is nice and fine, cover it with water again, and leave it somewhere where it won't be moved so that it will settle. Next day pour off the water, and any other foreign bodies that have floated to the top. Leave your clay to dry a little until it looks and feels as moist as Plasticine, set some aside on a plate to dry out completely (I'll tell you why in a minute) and bring the rest inside. Your clay needs *kneading* first, to distribute the moisture and get rid of any remaining lumps. Take a good-size hunk, put it on a piece of board, and roll it and pound it; make it into sausage shapes and flatten them again, until you can feel it is ready for modelling. Now you can use it just like Plasticine, making pots by rolling it into long sausages and then coiling it round and up, by rolling it out with a milk bottle into slab shapes, then cutting them and fitting them together, or simply by moulding it in your hands (see p. 82).

Adding a pattern

When you have made your pots you can decorate them, if you want to, with a raised pattern in this way. Take that spare clay I told you to put out to dry, crush it to a powder with the milk bottle-rolling pin, mix it with some water and use it as *slip* (as it is called by potters) to trail a pattern over the jar or basin, or to act as a 'glue' to stick a handle on a cup. You may be lucky enough to have a kiln at school which you can use for firing your pots so that they become really hard, but if you haven't you will just have to do what they did in Roman times – make your own.

How to make your kiln

Find a grassy corner of the garden that 'doesn't matter' (you'll soon see why!), cut a square of turf off with a spade and put it on one side, then dig a nice deep square hole beneath. If you haven't any peat (children with gardening parents will probably find some around, somewhere), buy a small sack from a gardening shop. Now build yourself a little fire in the bottom of the hole using twigs and dry paper and, if you like, a few pieces of charcoal. When it is well alight, put some peat on top of it to keep it going, a nice thick layer.

Fill your clay pots carefully with peat too (it is very light, and crumbles easily between your fingers)

The slab method; roll out the clay with a milk bottle, cut it into slab shapes and fit them together into a pot.

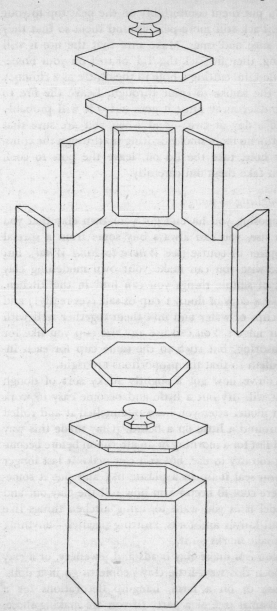

then put them comfortably on the peat top to your
fire. Pack still more peat around them so that they
are nice and snug. Make sure that the fire is still
going, then fit back the 'lid' of turf on your home-
made kiln, cutting a hole in the centre as a chimney
for the smoke to come through. Leave the fire to
smoulder away until it goes out – it will probably
take a day or two – and when you are sure that
there's no more smoke drifting up through the chimney hole, take the lid off, leave the pots to cool,
then take them out carefully.

Modelling in dough

Supposing you haven't got your own clay that you
can use, you can always buy some from a special
supplier of course (see *Where to Find What*), but
otherwise you can make your own modelling clay
out of simple things you can find in the kitchen.
Take 4 cups of flour, 1 cup of salt (yes really!) and
$1\frac{1}{2}$ cups of water and mix them together well with
your fingers. You can use any size cup you like for
measuring, but stick to the same cup for each in-
gredient so that the proportions are right.

You've now got a slightly sticky sort of dough
that will dry out a little and become easy to work
and model after you have pummelled it and rolled
it around a little on a board. (Clay made this way
will last for a morning or an afternoon before becom-
ing too dry to use, but you can make it last longer
if you seal it up in a plastic bag and put it somewhere cool to keep.) You now roll the clay out and
model it as you want to, using kitchen things like
small knives and forks, knitting needles – anything
to make marks on it.

You can make clay beads and jewellery, or a clay
brooch this way, little clay people to go in a dolls'
house or on a farm, hang-up decorations for a
Christmas tree or a party (if you are making those,

push a paper-clip or a hairpin in the back while the clay is still soft, to hang them up by). Once you've got your clay modelled the way you want it, put it on a baking tray very carefully, and bake it in the oven for an hour at a temperature of 350°F (Mark 4). After the hour is up, take a look at them – small figures will be 'fired' by then; if you have made something large it may take a little longer.

Finishing touches

When your figures are ready, let them cool and then decorate them – you can use poster or acrylic colour or, if you haven't any paints, felt-tipped pens will do. Afterwards, if you want to make them stronger and more permanent with a glossy finish, you can varnish them with any clear kind of varnish – even nail varnish. You can bake decorations into your figures if you want to – buttons or beads pressed into the clay when it is still soft will stay put after their treatment in the oven, but don't use plastic things or they will almost certainly melt.

Carving in salt

Two final modelling things you can do in the kitchen – a block of kitchen salt, the old-fashioned kind, is very good to practise carving on since it is not difficult to chip away – and it's the cheapest and easiest way to find out whether you like doing carving (see drawing on p. 88). If you keep it clean and put the crumpled bits into a plastic bag, your mother is not likely to object. Later on, if you find that carving from blocks interests you, you can buy some plaster of Paris, mix it to a cream, pour it into a cardboard box, and tear away the cardboard when it has dried, leaving you a block shape to work on.

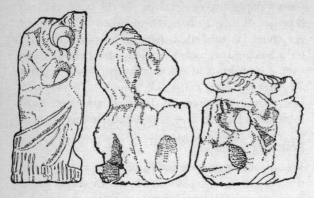

An ordinary block of kitchen salt can be carved into all sorts of interesting shapes.

Modelling in wax

The other kind of modelling you can do in the kitchen is with wax. Most people have a few old candle stubs around the house somewhere or other, left over from Christmas or power cuts. Put them in a basin together and melt them down in a bowl in a saucepan of water, as you did with the chocolate for cake making. If there are several colours and you stir them, you get a marbled effect. If you can't find anything but white candle stubs, try to cadge an old lipstick off your mother and melt that down with them – stir well and you'll have scarlet candle wax. Your wax is now ready for use.

Make a home-made wick by cutting a piece of fluffy-ish string to the right length, find an interesting shaped container – it could be anything, a tin, an egg-cup – get someone to hold the wick upright while you pour the wax around it, and you will have made yourself a brand new candle. Alternatively you can make the wax into a block in the way I described for plaster of Paris, then carve it into an interesting shape – but don't forget to put the wick in in the first place if you want to use it as a candle later on.

Tie and dye

What else can you do in the kitchen? 'Tie and dye', of course – a good way of jazzing up an old school T-shirt, a pair of faded jeans or simply a handkerchief or a piece of cloth you want to make up into something else. Tie and dye is not all that complicated to do, and you can turn out some wonderful patterns in it, but it is inclined to be a messy process, so be warned in advance. Put lots of newspaper on the floor, don't let the dye get anywhere where it might stain, and wear household gloves, if you can borrow some, to stop all that scrubbing of fingernails afterwards. If you have an automatic washing machine you *might* be able to do your dyeing in that, in which case it is a much cleaner and easier process – your mother will tell you if you can or not. If not you will need a very large saucepan – things called preserving pans that are used for jam making are ideal, if your mother has an old one.

The idea of 'tie and dye' is that you do something called 'resist dyeing' of the cloth. You take your fabric and knot it very tightly indeed, or tie it by winding twine round it, so that crumpled patches of it don't get soaked in the dye at all, while the rest change colour – and when you undo your knots you are left with a pattern in two colours. There's no end to what you can do with 'tie and dye' – you can go on, for instance, to re-knot and dye the fabric again, so that a second pattern and a second colour appear.

Let's do something simple for a start – a handkerchief. It must be absolutely clean because any sort of grease, for instance, would 'resist' the colour you are going to put on it (we'll use this fact in another kind of dyeing you might like to try, later on). Buy yourself some dye (see *Where to Find What*), read the instructions carefully, and then mix it up; you usually have to dissolve it in hot water. Now take your handkerchief and knot it very tightly in the middle, or at each corner, then put it into the dye, stirring it and 'cooking' it, as the instructions on the packet tell you.

Finally, rinse it carefully under a cold tap until no trace of the colour comes out. Hang it up to dry, then untie your knots and you'll find your handkerchief now has some interesting circular patterns on it. You use exactly the same method for dyeing a T-shirt this way (see diagrams below) – make as many knots as you want to or bind up sausages of fabric with string to get interesting shapes. You can do all sorts of other things, like tying pebbles inside the cloth for special spotty effects, once you've mastered the basic idea. Or you can concertina the fabric and then sew it in place to get a striped effect.

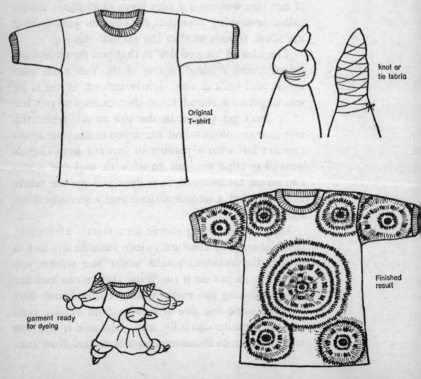

knot or tie fabric

Original T-shirt

garment ready for dyeing

Finished result

Simple batik dyeing

'Tie and dye' is not the only way of making patterns on fabric. You can use the fact I told you about – that the fabric must not be dirty or greasy or the dye won't take, to do other kinds of resist dyeing. Try dripping wax on to a piece of fabric, for instance (just light a candle and let it drip, or move it around using it like a paint-brush), then dip the cloth in cold water dye and see what effect you get – if you deliberately crack the wax before dyeing, you will get a very interesting marbled effect. If you haven't any wax, you can do the same sort of thing with flour and water paste – boil some up, paint it on, and leave it to dry before you dye. Afterwards you can easily wash the flour paste out. To take away wax, flake off as many loose pieces as you can and get rid of the rest by putting the fabric between two sheets of newspaper and going over it with a very hot iron.

Making your own dyes

If you're really interested in fabric printing, then you ought to make up some of your own dyes – it's much more fun than using bought ones, it's cheaper too, and the colours are much softer and more interesting. Find out from your history books what they used in olden times for dyeing their clothes – the woad that the ancient Britons used to paint themselves blue was used for dyeing cloth, too. It comes from a plant called dyer's woad, that has, strangely enough, yellow flowers, and it looks just like shepherd's purse (see p. 92). Its official name is *Isatis tinctoria*, it likes chalky or clay soil and you might recognize it by its funny droopy pods, each of which only contains one seed. You can buy seed if you want to (see *Where to Find What*).

You can also make your own dyes from the bark of trees, from berries, from lichen or, more easily, from

the juice of blackberries or elderberries. Try different things and see what you get. If you want the dye to stay permanent, though, you will need some alum from the chemist – stir 75 g alum into 1 litre of water to 'fix' your colour afterwards.

Left:
Elderberries yield a rich purple dye.

Right:
Isatis tinctoria, common dyer's woad, gives the blue dye used by the ancient Britons.

Flour-and-water paste

If you find yourself without any glue, you can make a perfectly good flour-and-water paste by simply mixing flour and water together until it makes a thick cream. A stronger paste can be made by boiling the mixture for two minutes, then letting it cool, beating it all the time with a wooden spoon so that it doesn't form a disgusting-looking skin over the top.

Ginger beer

Finally, if you feel like a refreshing drink, how about making your own ginger beer? Boil up 3 litres of cold water, put one sliced lemon, a pinch of cream of tartar, just over 200 g sugar, 12 g bruised ginger (from the chemist) into a heat-proof jar. Pour the water over them and then, when it has cooled to just luke-warm heat, stir in 12 g dried yeast that has been mixed to a paste with a little water. Cover your jar and leave it for 24 hours, somewhere warm. Skim the froth off the top, and it's ready to drink!

Ideas for Your Party

The best kind of parties that anyone can give, or go to, are those that are worked out well in advance. There's not much point in inviting a lot of people round unless you've organized something for them to do. How many times have you been to a party, for instance, where all the boys fought each other and rolled on the floor while the girls sat in the corner giggling, and no one enjoyed anything very much except the food? So work out a theme, an idea for the afternoon or evening; that way you're sure to have a good time.

Getting ready for a party is very important. First of all persuade your parents to let you clear most of the furniture out of the room where the action will be going on, especially things like ornaments that get knocked off shelves so easily, and delicate chairs. Two fat people once sat down together, at the same moment, on a prize sofa of mine at a party I gave – and it broke in half in the middle. I'm not suggesting you're going to have fat people along, but lots of children are bouncers – when they get excited they tend to jump up and down on the furniture, and that way things get knocked over and broken very easily.

Turning a garage into a submarine

One of the best places to have a party, in my opinion, is a garage – provided it's not cluttered up with garden tools. It's better than having it in the garden because plants can get trampled on and squashed and it's almost as good as having a party in the cellar, if you have one. Properly decorated, a garage can become anything from a cave, an undersea scene, a ghost house to a space ship. It also makes a good discothèque if you've got an electric socket in there to take a lead from a record-player. All you need, in fact, is the empty space, lots of coloured paper, perhaps one or two coloured lights (you can buy coloured light-bulbs very easily in electrical shops) and some tinfoil for glitter. An undersea scene, for instance, is easily made by taping lengths of sea-blue crêpe paper to the walls, then pasting cut-out fish and plants on it – to save money you could simply cut 'portholes' of blue crêpe paper, with fish stuck on it, then you have the effect of being in a submarine looking out.

If you're having the party away from the house, it will save a lot of time and trouble if each guest has his or her own party kit – a small cardboard cake box with a paper hat, some sandwiches, jelly and cake in it. That way it saves washing up afterwards ... a point that goes down well with mothers who tend to object to the extra work.

Party on the move

A kind of party that takes you away from home altogether is the moving party, which is meant to be held in summer. Each guest is given a 'Rover' bus ticket (there are Red Rovers, Green Rovers, all kinds of different special bus excursion tickets you can get, according to where you live) and a bag of food. Guests go off in pairs and the object of the game is to see who manages to get the furthest, and back again, or who has covered the largest mileage (the winner in that case may have simply gone round and round in small circles). For this you all need notebooks and pencils so that you can keep a log. If you do this kind of excursion in a big town, it's funny to find how often each pair of party people finds themselves meeting up with some of the others as they change buses.

Dressing up parties

A lot of people think that 'fancy dress' parties are boring, and so they are if the party turns out to be nothing more than a competition to see who is the best dressed. For there's always someone who cheats

Strips of coloured Sellotape make the face and fringed black tissue paper the hair of this party balloon.

by getting their parents to make something specially for them, or who has an expensive costume kept specially for occasions like this. It's more interesting to work up a theme and tell everyone beforehand. You could say, for instance, that they must come dressed as a character out of a TV programme, or a comic, or as a monster. Two people together can make a marvellous monster along the lines of a pantomime horse, but more frightening. It could be two-headed, for instance, and four-legged. A simple dress-up idea that doesn't present too many problems over clothes is to ask everyone to come dressed as one or other of their parents – the results can be very funny, though not for the parents concerned!

Instant fancy dress

To make the fancy dress more of a challenge you can collect a quantity of crêpe paper, newspaper, old clothes, pins and oddments and get your guests to make up their fancy dress on the spot, letting them help themselves to the props as they arrive. This does at least cut out all the more usual costumes and decreases the number of pirate kings, Arabs and princesses.

If, on the other hand, you're suddenly asked to

go to a fancy-dress party and haven't got anything handy to wear, a girl can turn herself into a doll very quickly by borrowing make-up from her mother for an artificial-looking face, and a wig, too, if there is one around. Then all she has to do is wear her best dress and walk rather stiffly as though she is a wind-up toy. A boy can quite simply get hold of a lot of newspaper, make a hat out of one sheet and pin the rest to him in pages, and then simply announce that he is the *Daily Whatever-it-is*. Or he can go as a bank robber, with a stocking over his head.

Animal farm party

If you haven't held one before, an animal farm party is a great success, and gives everyone a chance to see just how inventive he can be. You ask each guest to bring an 'animal' with them that they have made themselves, from things found around the house. It can be a real animal or a fictional one, like a dragon or the gryphon from *Alice in Wonderland*. It can be made from anything you like but nothing must be bought specially; the room in which the party is being held could be disguised as a zoo, with pens made from things like fireguards to keep the animals in.

Making the animals

How to make the animals? That's up to you. You can make a boa constrictor, for instance, from old washing-up liquid containers strung together and painted, or a smaller snake from the centres of toilet rolls on string.

An easy one is the hobby-horse, and you can make it this way. You need an old sock, some scraps of coloured fabric or paper and a walking-stick, preferably one with a straight, not a hooked, handle, but it must have a handle of some kind. Stuff the sock

firmly with crumpled-up newspaper, packing it in
quite tightly. This is the head of your hobby-horse.
The sock's toe is the horse's nose, the heel is the
back of its head and the ribbed edge is the neck.
Cut two narrow strips of fabric or paper and glue
them in place at the toe end of the mouth (Copydex glue is fine, or you could just use tacking
stitches). Cut two circles now for eyes and put them
each side of the sock just forward of the heel. Now
cut two triangles of fabric or paper as near as possible in colour to the shade of the sock, and fix them,
perked up, on top of the sock heel for ears. The
sock won't look like a sock any more, but quite a
convincing horse's head. Pull the stuffed sock well
down over the handle of your walking-stick, fix it
in place with tightly-wound string or elastic bands
and you're ready to go. (For this and other ideas for
making animals, see drawing on p. 95.)

A party dragon

A more complicated animal, and one that is best for
the party host to make, since it involves lugging
something heavy around, is a party dragon. For this
you need one of those cylinder vacuum cleaners, the
kind with a long hose and, I might add, a mother
who is willing to lend it to you. You'll also need
some stiff:sh paper – a large supermarket bag would
do, and some cardboard.

If you are lucky enough to find a large bag the
length of the cleaner's cylinder then this is what you
do – simply cut open the bottom and slide it over
the cylinder using sticky tape to make it fit, then
decorate it with spots or other dragon-like decorations (see p. 95). If you're having to use a length of
paper instead, then fit it round the cylinder and
then sticky tape it into a tube. The hose part of the
vacuum cleaner, which is the dragon's neck, can be
left just as it is, or wrapped round spirally with

crêpe paper – or you could cut the foot off an old nylon stocking and pull that over it for a cover (come to think of it, you might need more than one stocking though).

Put the snout-like attachment on the end of the hose, then make yourself a dragon's head any way you please – the easiest way I know is to draw a dragon's head side view, twice over, cut it out twice in stiff cardboard, fasten it together above and below with sticky tape, then slide it over the hose. Another idea is to find a small cardboard box which you can push the hose and snout through, then decorate. You mustn't cover the slit which sucks the air in whatever you do, but you're not likely to make this mistake since it has become the dragon's mouth. The same goes for the body, too – don't cover over anything on the dragon so that people can feed him with harmless things like pieces of cornflakes, and hear him purr, but watch that no one tries to ram anything fluffy in his mouth.

Pocket-sized animals for an animal farm party can be made quite easily out of vegetables – a plump potato can make a good pig, for instance. Anyway, those are a few ideas to go on with; the whole point of the party is the extraordinary animals that you think up for yourself.

Party hats

The kind that come in crackers are usually so flimsy that they tear as you are still trying to push them on your head, so it makes more sense to turn out some party hats of your own. The hat overleaf, left, can be made into lots of things once you have folded the basic shape. It could be a fisherman's hat, a fireman's hat or an Admiral's hat, for instance.

To make it you need a sheet of coloured paper longer than it is wide, about the size of a single page of a newspaper (it's a good idea to practise with

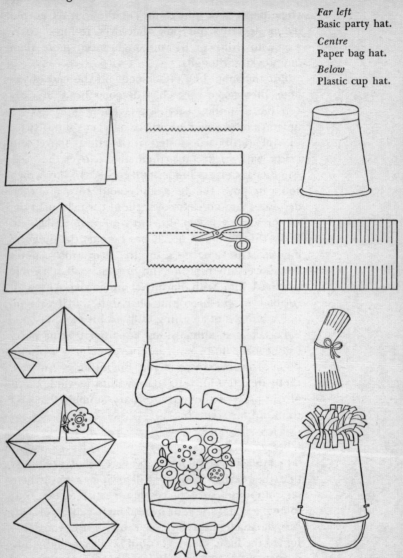

Far left
Basic party hat.

Centre
Paper bag hat.

Below
Plastic cup hat.

newspaper first, anyway). Fold the paper in half, across, then fold each folded corner down towards the centre so that the two points meet. Fold the bottom edge outwards on each side to form a cuff, and you have the basic triangular hat. To make it look more tidy you can fold over the protruding corners of the cuff and stick or pin them down. The hat is now ready to wear. If you want to turn it into a lifeboatman's hat simply turn it so one of the side folds is over your nose and fold the front half of the hat back. Otherwise you can decorate it with stick-ons, or slip paper pompons, flags or flowers into the folds.

Made from a drinking cup ...

Another kind of hat that girls seem to like in particular is made in five minutes out of a plastic or paper drinking cup, the kind you often drink out of at parties anyway. Paint the cup in bright colours (if it is waxed on the outside, try using acrylic colour or a felt-tipped pen) or stick coloured or patterned paper over it. Spear a small hole in each side right next to the rim, and thread narrow elastic or string through, knotting it at either end on the inside when it is the right length to slip under someone's chin.

This hat can be decorated in dozens of different ways – you could colour it royal blue, cut out a 'badge' from a piece of gold paper doyley and make it into a joke policeman's hat. Or you could put a paper brim on it, cut from a circle of cardboard and turn it into a Quaker's hat. Paint that version black and it makes a good witch's hat. You could also leave it white, cover it with paper flowers to make it look pretty or decorate it with a crêpe paper pompon made (see opposite) from a long strip of crêpe paper cut into a fringe along both long edges, rolled up, tied in the middle and turned back on itself.

... Or a paper bag

If you haven't any paper cups, an ordinary paper bag makes a good party hat too (see p. 100). Make sure though that it fits your head size before you start. The bag probably looks too tall on your head, and you may find you need to cut off about a third of its length. To strengthen it, bind the bottom edges with sticky tape: cut the tape into two lengths each the width of the bag. Lay one strip of tape on the table, put one edge of the bag on it so that it covers half the width of the tape, press down, then turn up the rest of the tape on to the inside. Repeat this on the other side.

Use sticky tape again to fasten two paper streamers, one on either side to tie under your chin, if you want to make it into a bonnet. Now paint a flower or a bird on the bag, or make an all-over pattern from a potato print. A plastic bag can make a good party hat, but you must be careful that it's either too small to slip accidentally over your face, or that it has ventilation holes in it, or you could just suffocate. A clear plastic bag makes a goldfish-bowl hat – you simply make some paper goldfish and stick them to the inside with a dab of glue, or suspend them on fine cotton which is fastened on the top folded edge, so that they look as if they are swimming round.

Paper lantern

Bought party decorations are all very fine, but sometimes if you want to give a special look to the room or perhaps have a special colour scheme like all black and white, it is difficult to find just what you want. Something that is very easy to make is a paper party lantern – you could string dozens of them from the ceiling. It's worth-while making these out of stiff paper so you can use them again and again.

Paper lanterns are easy to make and give an instant partyish look. For Christmas you could make them in gold or silver metallic paper. Or you could make patterned lanterns by decorating the paper before you cut them out.

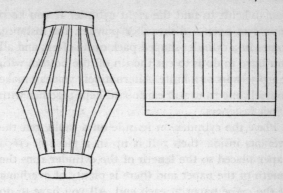

You need a rectangular sheet of paper, that is, longer than it is wide. Fold the paper in half, lengthwise, so that it looks even narrower and longer, then, with a ruler, sketch in a line 2·5 cm from the top along the cut, not the folded edge. Mark the folded edge of the paper with a series of dots about 10 mm apart. Take a sharp pair of scissors and cut in a straight line from each dot up towards the line you have sketched (you can see what I mean from the drawing above). Make sure you cut through both thicknesses of paper. Unfold your paper now, and curve round the short sides so that they meet and fasten at the top, the bottom and the middle with sticky tape. Make two small holes in each side of the top to take a piece of knotted string to hang the lantern up.

Giant cracker

If you're having a present hand-out at your party, and the items that your guests are going to get are smallish, you can pack them all into a giant cracker that is opened by a tug-of-war. The most important part of the cracker is a cylinder of cardboard in the centre in which all the presents are put. It's not *that* difficult to find the right cylinder if you keep your eyes open – dishwasher powder, for instance, comes in a cylinder-shaped pack quite often, and all you have to do is to cut the tin off the bottom with sharp scissors or a knife. Alternatively you can make yourself one from stiff cardboard kept together with paper fasteners.

Place the cylinder on its side on a table, put the presents inside, then roll it up in a piece of crêpe paper placed so the length of the cylinder runs the length of the paper and there is plenty of overhang of the crêpe paper at each end. All you have to do then is to finish off with the traditional cracker-like twist at either end of the cylinder, held in place with sticky tape. The guests divide into two teams, each team takes a crêpe paper end and pulls. The cracker bursts open, and they scramble for the presents.

Witches' party

There are plenty of times other than birthdays and Christmas for party giving, and a good one is a witches' party at Hallowe'en, on 31 October. If you can get hold of a pumpkin or a squash or even a very large swede, you can hollow out its inside and put a nightlight inside it, for a marvellous lantern with fang-like teeth. You might find you could use a giant marrow for this as well. Bobbing for apples is the traditional Hallowe'en game; for this you need plenty of newspaper on the floor or an old sheet or some plastic, because it involves a great deal of splashing. Apart from that your equipment is a washing-up bowl half full of water and some apples. Float the apples in the water and get each guest in turn to bob for them. The idea is for the player to try and pick the apple up with his teeth, with his hands tied behind his back. Another version of this, which is less messy, is to suspend the apples on a piece of string (thread the string through with a

darning needle, and knot it) and let each guest try
and take a bite.

A spooky game for Hallowe'en which needs a few
props and plenty of imagination is 'Old Tom is
Dead'. Old Tom, in our family, is usually a cat. The
narrator organizes himself with the props that he
needs (more about this in a minute), makes the rest
of the guests sit round in a circle, and puts out the
light. He speaks in a charming voice. 'Old Tom is
dead,' says the narrator, making up some suitably
gory story, 'Here are his eyes ...' and he passes
round two grapes (it's amazing how like eyes they
feel, in the dark). 'Here is his nose ...' and he passes
round a piece of carrot ... 'Here is his fur ...' and
he passes round a fur collar. You can also have
Tom's claws (pieces of bent paper-clip), his kidneys
(they could be real kidneys if your mother has any
in stock) and so on. Grown-ups don't particularly
like this game, but children do.

April Fool's Day is a good day for a party, too –
I went to one once when the marvellous meringue
on top of the cake turned out to be shaving cream
squirted out of an Aerosol!

'Pass the Parcel'

Two easy party games that can be whipped up
quickly with the aid of some newspapers are 'Pass
the Parcel' and 'Railway Carriages'. Pass the Parcel
is easy, it's just another version of musical chairs.
Choose some small object for a prize – a bar of chocolate is fine – and wrap it up with paper and string
again and again, until it has become a giant parcel.
You stand in a circle, put on a record and give
someone the job of stopping the music every so
often. Every time the music stops, whoever holds the
the parcel unwraps as much paper as he can before
the music starts up again. Whoever unwraps the
last piece has the chocolate.

'Railway Carriages'

This game always causes a riot. You will need to do a bit of preparation. Save up at least a week's supply of your daily paper, then make up a newspaper for each party guest with all the days and the pages shuffled. In other words, each person has a front cover but inside, in the wrong order, are pages from different days of the week. Now place a chair for each person in two rows facing, so close together that when you all sit down you are jammed side by side, sitting with your knees touching, just as if you were in a crowded railway carriage. To make it even more cramped you can place the chairs against the wall at one end. If the numbers are uneven, make the odd person stand in the middle of the row.

At the word go, everyone has to try to get his newspaper in the right order as quickly as possible, swopping pieces with his neighbours, grabbing others. If he has Monday's front cover, for instance, he must end up with all the Monday pages inside in the right order. The result is total panic with people jumping up and down and snatching at other people's pages. It's great fun both to play and to watch.

Pencil and Paper

It's amazing what you can do with paper. You can fold it, mould it, write or paint on it, build things with it, use it for all sorts of games. And the joy of it is that it is so cheap – there is always some paper around the house to play with, even if it is only yesterday's newspaper. In fact as long as you have some sort of paper to hand you need never be bored.

Origami

The simplest way of making things from paper is just to fold it into shapes. The best-known way of doing this comes from Japan and is called Origami, and it has become so popular that there are lots of books you can buy on that subject alone. To give you an idea how it is done, I'll show you how to fold an Origami boat (see diagrams overleaf).

My daughter loves doing Origami, and covers the floor of her bedroom with pieces of half-folded Origami things. But I must be honest and say (possibly because I have to clear them up afterwards!) that I am not keen on Origami myself. It can be quite complicated to do, and the result is not always worth it – I'm always getting into trouble for not recognizing that the tortured piece of paper waved under my nose is meant to be an owl or a frog. I think that paper sculpture is easier to do, and the results are more worthwhile. And if you are not very good at following folding directions you'll prefer paper sculpture, too. Anyway, let's try some.

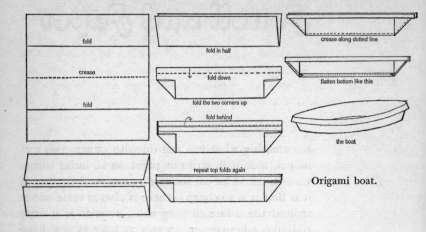

Origami boat.

Paper sculpture

Cut out the shape of a man in stiff paper, and draw in some features and some clothes. Now fold your figure in half, lengthwise, right down the middle. Immediately, two things happen – you can stand him up, and he looks quite lifelike because he now has more than one dimension. But you don't have to stop here. Now you can give another suit of clothes to make him even more real. Trace round his body on to another piece of paper, add the outline of paper tabs at his shoulders and his waist, or cut out a loop for his head to go through – then you can make him a paper tunic that you can fit on to him (with the tabs or the loop) and he looks still more real. You can give him a paper hat, too – just cut out a hat shape to fit his head, cut a slit in it where the brim joins the crown, one that doesn't go quite to the outer edges at each end, and then slip his head through. You could, if you wanted to, cut a hat *and* beard out all in one and slip them over his head.

A woman is even easier to do, for you can give her slip-on hairstyles, lots of skirts, and even a shawl to go round her shoulders, all from cut-out paper. The arms of your paper figure can be curled round by drawing a knife blade along them, or you can cut out the arms separately and glue them to the body at the back.

All the king's men

You can make splendid soldiers out of brown paper and give them pieces of armour cut out in white. You can bend one hand under and make it hold a shield or you can give them crowns and make them into medieval kings. You can cut out a man wearing a cloak, and then put arms coming through slits in it. Having done all this, you can be still more ambitious and make a horse. Use the centre of a toilet roll as the base for its body, then drape stiff paper folded double and cut out in the shape of its body and legs, over the roll, and glue it in place. You can then glue on a head and neck and a tail, cut double and folded in half. And having done this you can cut a bow-legged figure to sit on it. Then you can add paper reins for him to hold and a decorated harness for the horse to wear.

Fir trees and mobiles

You can make a handsome paper fir tree (it makes a good Christmas decoration, too) by making a cone of paper 15 cm high, then making a very long strip – at least 1·2 m long by 5 cm wide, from lengths of paper taped together end to end, then cut into a fringe. Wind your fringed strip round the cone, starting at the point at the top and curving round to the bottom, sticking it in place as you go. Paper can be folded and cut too into weird and wonderful animal shapes and suspended with cottom from a wire coat hanger to make marvellous mobiles.

The main thing to remember with anything you do with paper sculpture is that the more times you fold the paper, the stronger and more rigid it becomes.

Paper piggy bank

A paper pig is easy to make, and you can use it to keep your pocket money in. Cut out a piece of stiff paper 12 cm long by 20 cm wide. Cut a slit right in the middle for the money to go in, then roll the 20-cm-side round into a cylinder and tape it in place. Measure the diameter of your cylinder at either end (in other words, its measurement across the circle) and you will find it is about 6 cm depending on how much you have overlapped the paper. Using a compass, draw two circles of this size from a piece of card and tape them in place at either end. Make four short legs from folded pieces of card taped on to each corner on the underside of your 'pig' (it should be stood slit-side uppermost), then cut out a curly tail from paper and stick in the centre of one end, two flaps for ears at the other and a tiny circle of cardboard for the nose. Draw in the eyes and he is ready for use.

Papier-mâché

What else can you do with paper? You can use it for modelling. Papier-mâché is, as the French words say, mashed-up paper, usually newspaper, and you can use it in several ways. Indeed, the Victorians were so fond of papier-mâché, and so good at making it that they actually made light pieces of furniture from it. Basically, it is torn-up pieces of paper that have been thoroughly soaked in water for a day or so, then used in one of two ways: either glued on top of each other in layers over some shape that is used as a mould, or mashed up in glue and crushed into a clay-like pulp that can be modelled and moulded in your hands to any shape you want.

First you'll need a lot of old newspapers and a large bowl. Tear the paper into pieces about 4 cm square (the exact size doesn't matter, the larger the thing you are making, the larger the pieces can be), then leave them to soak in a bowl of water. They should ideally be left for two or three days, but if you are in a hurry you can short-cut things by using hot water instead of cold, because it penetrates the paper more quickly. Drain off the water, press the pieces lightly and then you are ready to start work. You'll need to make up a large bowl of paste. Flour and water will do (make it so that it looks like thick cream) but wallpaper paste is best: it dries more quickly and becomes invisible.

Start off by making a simple bowl this way. Choose something for the mould – any sort of small bowl that is not likely to be wanted for a day or two will do – and carefully cover it with pieces of paper that have been soaked in water, so that they overlap each other slightly and so that none of the bowl can be seen. Having patted them carefully in place, brush them over with paste, then apply another layer of paper, again making sure that the first layer is completely coated. Then follow with a third layer, and so on, until the bowl has been coated with at least 4 or 5 layers of torn-up paper. Now all you have to do is to put it somewhere warm to dry – you'll find this will take a day or so, and it is important not to touch it meantime or the shape will be spoiled.

When it is completely dry you will find you can lift the papier-mâché bowl off its original mould and it just needs finishing. Trim off any rough edges with a sharp pair of scissors, paint the papier-mâché bowl inside and out in a bright colour and, when that has dried, give it several coats of clear varnish to strengthen and waterproof it.

This same system can be used to make puppets' or dolls' heads. But in this case you make your mould out of plasticine or plaster, then stick the paper on that – remember, though, that the first layer must be of paper that has been just moistened with water, not glue or you'll never get it off the mould.

Modelling in papier-mâché

Here is another way that you can use papier-mâché; for modelling without a mould. In this case you press the paper as free from water as you can (you can use a colander or sieve for the job) then soak it again in paste and drain it once more. For this particular type of modelling you can use some paper tissues among the newspaper to help keep it soft. Solid heads or figures made from moulded papier-mâché in this way will take a long time to dry, and it is important not to put them in an oven nor anywhere warm, or they will tend to crack on the outside while the inside is still wet. But once they have dried out they will become very hard indeed. (See picture below.)

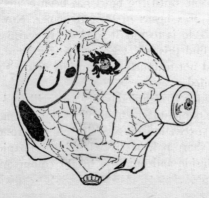

Papier-mâché pig. The snout has been made from a yoghurt pot and cardboard ears have been added.

As the turntable whirls faster and faster, the colours of the spectrum 'disappear'.

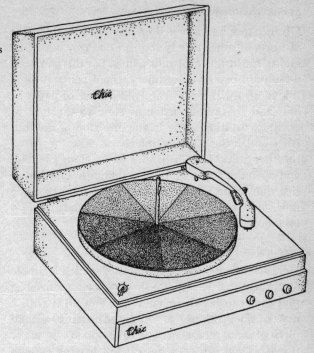

Whirling colour disc

Do you know how to make colours disappear? This is very easy if you have a stiffish sheet of paper you can make into the shape of a gramophone record (the simplest thing to do is to use a record as a pattern, draw round it and punch a hole through the middle), then divide it into seven sections and colour them in this order – red, orange, yellow, green, blue, indigo and purple. Now put your colour 'record' on the turntable and turn the record player on – as it gets faster and faster you'll be surprised to find that instead of seeing the colours, the disc appears to be just plain white – this is a simple experiment to prove that white light is, in fact, made up of a spectrum of colours, something that you may have already learned at school. (See drawing above.)

Spooky handwriting

Given paper and a pencil or pen and ink, there are all sorts of other things you can do. You can make ghosts, for instance, of your names. For this you need a fountain pen or an ordinary school pen and some ink (a Biro will not work). Fold a piece of paper in half and write your name as close to the fold as possible, running along in the direction of the fold itself and using a lot of ink. Now close the paper together quickly, and run your finger along the fold, and open the paper again. You'll find that instead of just your name, you have a funny skeleton-like shape now, and that is the ghost of your handwriting – everyone's is different.

'Feelies'

Here's another game called 'Feelies', which is simple to arrange if anyone has a shoe-bag or a sponge-bag that they can lay their hands on. You fill it with a mass of small things – a button for instance, a small piece of soap, a tape-measure, a teaspoon – as many things as you can cram into it but leaving enough space for them to move around a little. Tie up the

An assortment of small objects is put in a bag and passed round for the players to identify by feel.

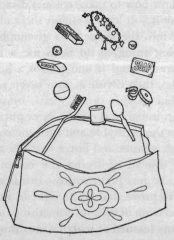

neck of the bag tightly and pass it around to each
person in turn who is given up to the count of
twenty to feel the bag, then write down what is in
it. Whoever identifies the most objects correctly is
the winner. (See drawing opposite.)

Agony column

A crazy game to play with pencils and paper is
Agony Column. You've seen those question-and-
answer columns in newspapers and magazines,
haven't you – things like 'My child doesn't under-
stand me, what shall I do?', with an answer by an
expert. *You* make up a series of questions, the
crazier the better, silly things like 'My dog has suddenly turned mauve, how shall I deal with the
situation?' while someone else sits writing silly
answers – to questions that he or she has not seen.
Each question and each answer is written on a
separate sheet of paper and put face down on the
table. The questioner picks up each of the questions
and reads them out, then after each question the
answerer reads his answer (which will have nothing
to do with the question at all, really). You can
imagine the results!

Squiggly outlines

A thing you can do on your own if you can find a
big sheet of paper is to make a design out of drawing
round ordinary objects such as a key, a pair of
scissors, a spoon and so on. Don't worry about them
overlapping – it'll make your design all the more
interesting (see example on p. 116).

Coded messages

Finally, when you're playing around with paper and
pencil, don't forget the fun of making up your own
codes, so that you can send messages to each other
without anyone ever knowing what you've said. The

Drawing round
objects: see
Squiggly Outlines,
opposite.

simplest code you can do is to simply turn the
alphabet the other way round so, for A you write Z,
and so on – then you get a message like this: WL BLF
HVV DSZG R NVZM? But that is a code that lots of
people know and is quite easy to crack. However,
you can make it much more difficult immediately
by slipping the letters along one, so that Z is B instead of A, and Y is C. That way you find that two
letters – 3 and N – remain the same, which adds to
the confusion. You then end up with something
like this: XM CMG IWW ETAH S OWAN?

You can make very personal secret codes if you
take a large piece of cardboard and cut square
holes in it here and there – if you're going to write
to someone you'll need two pieces of card each with
holes in exactly the same place. You then put your
card over a piece of writing-paper, write out your
message, then lift the card off – and the letters will
be scattered about all over the paper. To confuse
your enemies, all you do is to write more letters –
real words or absolute gobbledygook in between
your original message, so that the page is a hopeless
jumble. The only person who can read the real
message then is the one who has a matching card.

On the Move

Travelling can be very exciting or very boring, depending on where you are going, of course, and what you are travelling in. The most exciting kind of travelling for me is to get my first sight of the French coast when crossing the Channel in a ship. The worst kind of travelling, from my point of view, is sitting waiting in an airport departure lounge, having been told that my plane has been delayed for two hours – or worse (once I was told my plane had been delayed for two *days*!).

Things to take on a journey

The main thing to remember is to have something ready in case you do find there are dull patches on your journey. No one should go anywhere, even on holiday, without taking *something* to do and something to read. Comics are rather a waste of money in this case, lovely though they may look on the bookstall, because in my family, at any rate, we find everyone has read them before they get to their destination. It's much better to go to your local bookshop instead and stock up with one or two paperbacks to read, ones you can swop around with each other. We find Spike Milligan's books go down well on journeys, so do books of puzzles, and historical stories too. Or you could be very worthy indeed and get a book about the place you are going to, so you know all about it before you get there.

You should never travel, either, without a thick pad of paper and a pencil or two (you can get good

Useful things to while away a boring journey include cards, games, puzzles and a scribbling pad.

thick pads at any shop that sells stationery for offices). It's good to have it with you for you might want to jot something down, or make a drawing; then there are all sorts of games you can play with a pencil and paper in your pocket. I always take a pocket chess set and a pack of cards, too. The chessmen are pushed into little holes in the cardboard, so they stay put when you close the box again, and you can continue your game later on. Don't forget to take a few sweets with you, too, if you are going abroad, but stick to wrapped rather than loose ones that can get sticky and *don't take chocolate* if you are going to a hot place like, say, Majorca, because it will certainly melt in your suitcase, in your hotel room, in the sun, and it never tastes quite the same again!

Games for the road

Travelling by car is fine, just so long as it doesn't make you feel sick. I used to get very ill in cars, in fact my father once trailed an iron chain behind us because someone told him that it was static electricity that was causing it, and that this would allow it to escape! However I found, and you may find too, that it was looking down to draw or to read that made me ill in cars – and you may find, if you suffer that way, that it's the same for you, too. If you *must* read, take my advice and look up at the scenery from time to time, that seems to stop the trouble. The best car games to play are those that

If you're going by car, see how many different animals you can spot on the way. The following creatures are hidden in this drawing: cow, horse, pig, sheep, dog, crow, frog, magpie, pheasant, hedgehog, duck, hen, owl, pigeon, snake, snail, rabbit.

use the journey in some way or other, like 'Animal,
Vegetable and Mineral', for instance. You really
need three people to play it, but if you are the only
passenger (the driver can't very well join in!) you
can still play by making three lists and seeing which
one wins. The idea is to collect the names of pubs,
according to whether they are *animal* (that means
humans, animals and birds), *vegetable* (that means
anything that grows, trees and big plants too) or
mineral (meaning any natural substance that isn't
animal or vegetable, such as a pebble or a piece of
metal). In other words, the Prince of Wales is an
animal, the Yew Tree is vegetable and the Blue
Anchor is mineral. At the end of the trip you see
who has the most (I'll give you a tip – usually the
animals win!). If there are just two of you in the
car you can simply divide it up between humans
and animals instead.

Collecting car brands is another easy one, provided you know what different makes of car look
like. One person takes Fords, another British Ley-
land, perhaps, and you see who has collected the
most by the time you reach the other end. If you've
got a road-map to look at and follow your route,
any journey by car becomes much more interesting
right away, for you can look out for places that
sound interesting and, if the map is an Ordnance
Survey one, or one with a lot of details on it, you
can try to spot things like Roman ruins, windmills
and tumuli that may be marked near your road.

You should be able to work out, too, on a long
journey, how many hours it will take you to get to
your destination. You could have a competition to
see who gets the nearest. If you are smart about it,
you'll take several different things into account
when totting up – the average speed at which the
car is going, by watching the speedometer, how many
towns you have to go through (towns always slow

you up), whether the countryside is very hilly or not, whether the roads are narrow winding ones or motorways – I reckon it takes twice as long at least to cover a distance on a really hilly, narrow road than it does on a motorway – see if I'm right.

Station bingo

A train journey is not usually as cramping as in a car because you can move about a bit, and, if you get in a carriage near the buffet car, with luck you'll find it has tables which make reading and writing easier. You can collect things on a train journey, take animals, for instance, that you spot from the window. It is also quite fun to play Station Bingo, a train game that needs some preparation beforehand. For this you need a train timetable, showing all the stations the train passes through, even if it does not stop at them all. Look up the line you are going on, make a list of all the stations between the point where you get on and get off. Now cut out the names, put them in a box and let each person pick out all but three, and write them down in a list in the order they came out of the box. Everyone should then end up with a different list of jumbled names of stations. On your journey, as the train passes each station on your list, you cross it off – and the first person to complete going through their list wins.

Shop monopoly

A long bus journey can be a stop-start affair, and it's not easy to get on with some reading if you're crammed in a seat. Here's where another journey game comes in – Shop Monopoly. Supposing you are going on one of those rather long, boring bus trips that takes you through one shopping-centre after another. Nowadays, there are so many chains of shops that you keep coming up against the same names – Sainsbury, Boots, Woolworth, and so on. You can use this fact to play a kind of Monopoly with them.

Make a list of the likely ones before you start, and award each shop chain a number according to how often you're likely to see them. Woolworth's would count as one or two, while Marks and Spencer's, which is rarer, would be about number ten. Then, on the journey, whoever spots the shop first gets the points that go with it, and you can see who gets the highest total in the end. You could play this game in a car, but you are usually moving too fast to get a look at the shops, whereas buses have to stop from time to time.

Fortune telling

You can tell each other's fortunes with ordinary cards if you make up your mind beforehand what each card will mean – the fortune bit comes in with the element of chance on which card you will turn up after you have shuffled them. The Ace of Spades always means bad news, the Ace of Hearts love. A King means that something important is going to happen to you, a Queen means you will have good luck, the Jack or Knave means the arrival of a stranger in your life. You can also ask the cards questions which require a number in the answer and see what you get. Like 'How many children will I have when I marry?' – I only hope you don't turn up Eight or Nine!

Heads, bodies and legs

Here's an old favourite for people who like drawing. You play it like Consequences too – everyone draws the head of something – bird, animal, flower, robot, on his or her piece of paper, folds it over so that it doesn't show, but you can just see the bottom of the neck, then passes it on for someone else to add

Heads, Bodies and Legs is played like 'Consequences'; here are two examples of the sort of drawings you might end up with.

a body. You usually divide up into heads, bodies, legs and feet, passing it round each time. If you want to make the game longer, you can get each person to write a name for the animal, some title like a 'Drunk four-legged duck' for instance, *before* the papers are unfolded.

Just to remind you ...

Did you say don't know what Consequences is? I don't believe it, but just in case, here's a quick run-through of the game. You are telling a story. First you write down the name of your hero, fold the paper, pass it on, and write down the name of the heroine (it could be anyone from the Queen to the girl next door, whatever takes your fancy). Then you say where they met, and what each of them was wearing, folding the paper and passing it on all the time. Then you say what he said to her, and what she said to him, and finally what the consequence was – remember?

Odds and Ends

There's no end to the number of interesting things that you can make from odds and ends, and one of the best of them is a picture. So if you like the idea of making your own pictures or sculpture, even if you don't seem to be very good at it at school, it pays to have a go at home, using odds and ends found around the house instead of an easel and a brush. After all, Robert Rauschenberg, the famous American artist, makes a great deal of money out of doing just this. He was the first person to think of putting real things like Coca Cola bottles and stuffed birds on to his canvases, and all sorts of other things. In fact, when I went to his exhibition in London once, I went to sit on one of his pieces of sculpture, which wasn't really surprising since it was a real chair! Pictures and sculptures of this kind are very often done best by people who are not very good at drawing, but have a good sense of design, and plenty of ideas – is this you? Are you ready to go?

Pins and cotton art

Start off by making some pin pictures which look very arty indeed and very professional, but are quite easy to do. If you find you enjoy making pictures of this kind, you can do bigger, more permanent ones later on using nails and wooden board. You need a piece of very stiff card or some hardboard, wallboard or plywood (you might be lucky and find a few off-cuts around) and a box of pins. You also need at least one reel of cotton; the colour is up to you.

Press or hammer the pins into your base of cardboard or whatever, putting them anywhere you fancy – scattered all over the place or clustered into groups. Now take the reel of cotton, fasten one end to a pin nearest the corner and start winding the thread from one pin to another, zig-zagging backwards and forwards as you feel like it. Sometimes your mother has just one spool of cotton she is willing to part with, sometimes you may have several colours to use in turn. If you feel the picture is not colourful enough, you can always paint in some colour on to the card. You'll find your finished picture (which will, of course, be an abstract one) looks just like those you see sometimes in galleries specializing in modern art.

Pasta pictures

Another way to make an abstract picture is to stick pieces of uncooked pasta – spaghetti, macaroni or tuberoni – on to a sheet of coloured paper. You can buy all sorts of interesting pasta – short, fat pieces, shapes like shells, even stars and letters of the alphabet and you can find them in any grocer's shop that sells Italian food for a few pence a packet. You simply take your background piece of paper, 'paint' a pattern or a picture on it with glue (Copydex is best) and then sprinkle the pasta pieces over it. Leave it to dry, shake the paper, and the pasta will stay put where the glue is, leaving the rest of the paper bare.

There are plenty more ways of making pictures, ideas you can think up for yourself once you get off the railway track of only thinking in terms of painting and drawing. In the autumn, for instance, big brown leaves can be collected and dried, then stuck down on paper with clear glue and decorated afterwards with sequins and other glittery things, then varnished. Torn-up tissue paper makes good pictures, too. Old clock and watch parts or any small

pieces of flat machinery can be glued to board or
card to make marvellous patterns, while postage
stamps can be arranged in an interesting design.

Weird and wonderful collage

Another picture idea is collage, scenes made up from
scrap photographs, magazine pictures and pieces of
fabric or paper. You can build up the most weird
and wonderful scenes quite quickly, just with the
help of scissors and paste. Take a nice, tranquil-
looking picture of a house in a country setting, for
instance, the sort of thing you find in estate agents'
advertisements in magazines like *Country Life*. Now
look for an animal's face, or a hand that is far too
large in proportion. With scissors and paste you can
transform your country house picture into something from a horror comic – a house with a huge
hand coming up over the roof, or perhaps a pair
of giant eyes peering out through the window, or a
monster's head looking round the side. If you're
very clever about cutting out and sticking down the
pieces you can make it look quite real.

Miniature peep-shows

Talking of houses, large pictures of houses can also
be made into miniature peep-shows this way. First
cut out the windows so that you can see through,
then paste on a separate sheet of paper some tiny
scenes of what the house is like when you look in.
They could be interiors from house pictures in
magazines or you could go completely surrealist and
make them small jungle pictures instead. Paste a
cardboard frame on to the back of the house picture,
then fasten your interior panorama to the other side
of it, so that there is a little gap between the two
pictures. When you look into the windows of the
house, the scene inside will look a little three-
dimensional. If you want to, you can cut the win-

dows on three sides only, so they are still attached
and open and shut.

A funny kind of collage that always makes people
laugh is the one that is done on a theme. For instance, you can make a funny picture out of nothing
but eyes, noses and mouths cut from newspaper
photographs and arranged haphazardly all over
the paper; alternatively you can play heads, bodies
and legs, and have a lot of fun rearranging people.

Plastic bag pictures

Here's something else you can do. You will need
3 or 4 clear plastic bags of the same size, the kind
that your mother puts sandwiches in, and some
acrylic colour which comes in tubes. Acrylic colour
is well worth spending pocket money on, for you
can use it to paint on practically any surface at all,
including plastic, and it goes beautifully on plastic
bags. The idea is to paint a different picture in a
different colour on each bag, then sandwich the bags
together, so that you get a three-dimensional effect.
You need to stretch the bags out carefully on a
piece of cardboard, of course, when you've painted
them, and fasten them in place with drawing-pins.

Pop art

If you like Pop art, the kind of pictures that Andy
Warhol makes, for instance, then you can get rather
the same effect by colouring newspaper photographs
with poster paint. Film stars can be given ruby-red
lips, amazingly blue eyes and bright yellow hair.
These make good illustrations to put up on your
bedroom wall.

Pots that don't need firing

Making things with modelling clay (if you haven't
any clay, see how to make modelling dough in
Kitchen Cunning) is a very worthwhile thing to do,

especially now that you can buy clay that doesn't
need cooking in the oven (see *Where to Find What*).
You don't have to have a potter's wheel, either, for
making quite good-looking pots – just roll the clay
into a long, long snake, coil it round in a circle for
the bottom of the pot, then build up the sides by
coiling the snake round and round on itself. If you
don't like the ridges that are left, you can smooth
them over afterwards with a knife or finger (see
p. 82).

Try your hand at sculpture

Polystyrene packing material – that stuff that looks
like frozen white foam, and comes round television
sets and all sorts of big bulky household things –
can be carved to make some very interesting sculptures. You can cut it easily with scissors, too. Its
fantastic shapes can, with a little imagination, be
turned into moonscapes, anything you want, and
you can paint it afterwards with a high-gloss lacquer
paint; acrylic colours stick to it too. Polystyrene
people are easy to cut out, and easy to put features
on – you simply poke in the eyes with a pencil.

Another kind of sculpture which gives your imagination a real chance to get going is that made from
newspaper and sticky tape. You crush the newspaper into the shape that you want, then sticky-tape
it together before it has a chance to spring apart
again. Once you've got your figure fixed together,
you can make it more permanent by covering it
with a damp cloth soaked in plaster. There are more
ideas, you'll remember, for using paper in *Pencil
and Paper*.

Printing with a potato

Potato prints, like lino-cuts, make very interesting
patterns on paper or, if you buy some of the new
fabric paints that there are around, on T-shirts and

Potato prints are
fun to do, using
poster paint.

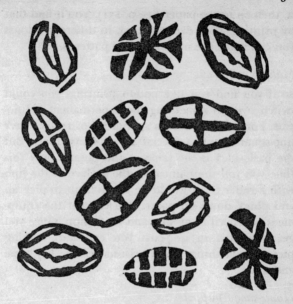

other clothes. Whether you use a potato or a piece
of lino for your printing, you cut them both in
exactly the same way. Whatever you cut away from
the printing block will appear white on the finished
pattern, whatever you leave will take the colour,
so you've got to think in reverse. Potato printing is
the easiest since you don't need special tools for it,
just a small sharp knife and a nice large potato.

Cut the potato in half so that you have a flat surface to work on, then, with a BB pencil, sketch in
very carefully the pattern that you want. When
you've got it right, cut away the potato around the
design very carefully to about a depth of 5 mm at
least, with a sharp knife. It's very important, if the
pattern is not going to turn out smudgy, to make
the cuts at right angles, not on the slope.

Now mix up some powder colour or poster paint
into a thick paste (a potato tends to be watery and
dilute things) and press your potato down on to

it, then on to the paper (see p. 131). You'll find that by printing, then over-printing, in different colours you can make the most fantastic patterns.

Making a lino-cut

So if you find you like potato printing, you could switch over to something more permanent – lino-cuts. For this you need a special kit of really heavy lino-squares, and a special set of sharp tools. But the basic idea is the same as the potato, only this time you roll the paint over the surface of the lino with a roller for it would be too difficult to pick up and plonk down on paint. You can get the equipment you need at an arts and craft shop. Once you get interested in lino-cuts you can start making pictures and things like Christmas cards. Try some and see.

Home-made puppets

People love playing with puppets. You can buy them, of course, ready made, from a shop, but the ones with the most character are the kind you make yourself from odds and ends – like the quickly-made cut-out puppet shown here, which is simply mounted on card and joined together with paper fasteners. I know someone who made a marvellous old peasant-woman puppet from the simplest thing – an apple she found in the corner of the larder. It had been there some time and had become wrinkled, and it reminded her of an old woman's face, so she gouged out two holes for the eyes, and pressed currants into them, marked in a mouth, then pushed the handle of a wooden spoon into the core for the body, then dressed it in a cloak made from an old dish-rag and a headscarf made from a handkerchief. It didn't last very long, of course, but it looked very real. In Austria and Germany they're very fond of making puppets and

Simplest of all
puppet, a drawing
or photograph
cut out, mounted
on card and
joined with paper
fasteners.

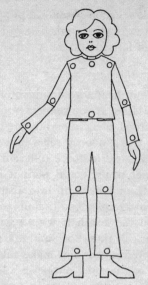

dolls out of nuts and fruit – raisins, pears, all sorts
of things.

Things to use for the head

Another unexpected thing that makes a good
puppet head is a bar of soap – you can carve it into
a face and then colour it with make-up. A ball of
wool makes a good temporary puppet head – I say
temporary because someone is bound to want it back
sooner or later – or you can use a tightly crumpled
newspaper kept in a ball shape with sticky tape,
then covered with a piece of nylon stocking. Plastic
containers make good puppets, too; you can cut a
washing-up liquid bottle into two pieces, one about
one-third long for the head, the other about two-
thirds long for the body. Choose one if you can that
has a plain side to it, so you can decorate it for the
face, otherwise you'll have to paint out the lettering. A ping-pong ball, pushed into a piece of nylon

stocking, makes a good base for a puppet head, too; it's much better than a tennis ball which tends to be too heavy and lolls about.

How to make the hair

Having got your head sorted out, you'll want to give it some hair. How? If you're lucky your mother may have a discarded hairpiece you can cut up. Straw makes good hair, so does raffia and so does wool which you can use in three different ways, Either leave the wool straight and plait it if the puppet is to be a girl, or knit it up into a square, wash it, then undo it again – you'll find you have curly 'hair', or you can brush it with a wire brush, the kind used for cleaning shoes, and make it look fuzzy and woolly. Wood shavings make splendid ringlets which you can glue on a puppet head. You can also make curls from brown paper this way: cut it into strips twice the length you want the finished hair to be, put each strip down on the table, hold the end nearest to you tightly and pull it up towards you, under the edge of a ruler. As it comes up it will curl. If that sounds too complicated, try winding it tightly round a pencil instead.

You can make your puppet faces look even more real if you add things to them. Those round-headed coloured pins make good beady eyes for animal puppets, while pieces of cork from old medicine bottles can be chiselled into noses for human ones.

Glove puppets

The easiest puppets to make to use are glove puppets, when the body is slipped over the operator's hand, and your little finger and your thumb become the puppet's arms. Puppet bodies are quite easy to make – the simplest one of all is made from an old oven-mitt if you can find one. All you do is cut off the thumb, if it has one, and make two holes in the sides for your little finger and your thumb to poke through and become the puppet's arms. The top of the mitt is sewn to the neck of the puppet head.

You can also use an oven-mitt as a pattern to cut out a puppet body, or you can make a slightly more elaborate one this way. Spread your hand out on a piece of paper, fingers out wide, and draw round it. Measure on your sketch the distance between the tip of your little finger and the tip of your thumb, and between the top of your middle finger and your wrist bone. Now cut out a piece of fabric the width of the first measurement you took and twice the second measurement (from middle finger to wrist). Fold the fabric in half, sideways. The centre of the folded edge is attached to the puppet's head, your finger and thumb poke out at the sides and you can, if you want to, cut away some of the fabric underneath to turn the cloth into a T shape, and give the puppet sleeves.

Make a two-way telephone

This is something you can make out of odds and ends if you have the kind of mind that can cope with rather fiddly things and doesn't get too impatient. You need 2 empty soup or baked-bean cans, some strong brown wrapping paper, some string, a roll of fine wire, milliners' or florists' wire is fine, and 2 matchsticks. First of all, take the bottoms off the cans with a can-opener (use the type that leaves the edges smooth), then damp the brown paper and stretch a piece over one end of each can, making sure it is as tight as you can get it, tying it tightly in place with string. Push one end of the wire through the centre of the brown paper in one tin, then tie the end to a matchstick, inside the can, so that it can't slip out again. Cut the wire off at about 5 m in length, then fix the other end to the other can in the same way.

To use your telephone, get as far away from each other as you can, each with a can in hand, keeping the wire as taut as possible, but not yanking so hard that it breaks the paper. Now one person talks into his can, while the other person holds his to his ear and listens. Try it, and see how you get on. I'm told you can also do this telephone trick by leaving the tin in the bottom of the cans, punching a small hole in it, and using string instead of wire, but I haven't tried it myself.

Making presents

Odds and ends come in very handy when Christmas and birthdays come round. If you are rather short on cash, it is often cheaper to make your relations presents instead of buying them something and, oddly enough, people like mothers and uncles and aunts often appreciate home-made presents all the more. Most children's annuals are full of ideas of things to make, so I won't bore you with too many, but here are one or two ideas you mightn't have heard of, that don't cost very much.

Handful-of-change paperweight

You can make a paperweight for your father or your uncle quite quickly and easily if you have a few coins lying around the house – loose change left from holidays abroad, for instance, or English coins that have gone out of usage. A paperweight needs to be heavy, that's the point of it, so you'll need quite a good handful of coins. You'll also need a cardboard beer mat, a cork mat or a piece of heavy cardboard, and some very strong glue (see *Where to Find What* section). Cover the top of the mat or the cardboard with glue, then stick down the largest coins you have, putting them close together, and arranging them so that their edges overlap the mat beneath. If any of the cardboard or cork shows at

This apparently casual heap of coins is stuck down on to a base.

the edge trim it off with a razor blade or nail scissors. Now fix more layers of coins on top of the first layer, using the same glue (see picture above). Make it look as casual as possible, as if you have put a handful of coins down on the table. It's interesting, actually, to see just how many people think they are simply a pile of coins, and go to pick one of them up.

Things made of orange peel 'leather'

You can make some really interesting belts and necklaces from the most unexpected thing – orange peel. For this you want to cut the fruit as carefully as you can, so that you get some nice large pieces of skin. When you've collected enough, cut the peel up into interesting shapes, squares, diamonds or circles, small ones if you're making a necklace, larger ones if it is to be a belt.

Make a small hole at either end of each piece very carefully with a small knitting-needle or a large darning-needle, depending on their size, then leave them in a warm dry place for several days to dry out. You'll find next time you look at them that the

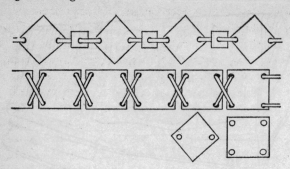

Orange peel
leather belt and
necklace.

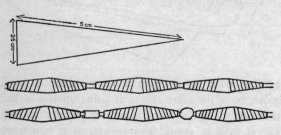

Making a string
of paper beads.

peel will have become quite tough and hard, just
like leather, and no one would dream it was orange.
You can now varnish them if you want to, or paint
them. When they've been decorated you simply
thread them together with wool, cord or leather
thonging to make them into a belt or necklace (see
diagram above).

Paper bead necklace

Another kind of jewellery can be made very quickly
and easily from coloured paper beads (see above).
This is one occasion when you don't want plain paper
to make them with, for it would be too uninteresting.
Gaudy-coloured wrapping paper or, best of all, the
coloured pages from comics are just fine for this.

Cut your paper into triangles 5 cm long on two
sides, 2·5 cm across the bottom (it's called an isosceles
triangle, if you do geometry at school). Cover the

wrong side of the paper pieces with paste (flour and water paste will do but the wallpaper kind is better) then roll them up as tightly as you can on a small-size knitting-needle, beginning at the base of each triangle and ending up at the point. Hold the 'bead' in place on the needle for a moment, then slip it off and leave it to dry. Later, when it is hard, you can varnish it, if you like, and thread it on wool or string. Vary your beads by inter-threading them with circular beads made from crushed aluminium foil and sausage-shaped pieces of macaroni.

Tissue tree table centre

In winter, when there aren't many flowers around, you can make a very pretty decorative tree out of paper tissues and odds and ends – it makes a good Christmas present too (see diagrams below). You need a short piece of broomstick, or a branch of the same thickness, some wire netting (often called chicken wire), a pair of thick gloves, one or two boxes of coloured paper tissues, and a flower pot to put it all in. First fill the flower pot with earth, and pack it down nice and tight, then crush the wire netting (this is where you need to wear the gloves) into a hard ball and ram it on to the piece of broomstick, squeezing the wire round it so that it will stay in place. Now push your tree skeleton into the flower pot, making sure that it is steady.

Paper rosebush.

To decorate the tree you simply undo the handkerchief tissues and poke them in, one by one into holes in the wire netting. Take each tissue by the centre and poke that piece in, so that you get a frilled effect from each handkerchief. You can add one or two paper flowers if you want to, working on until all the wire netting is covered. It makes a pretty table decoration and it has a practical use – when you're tired of it, you can use up all the tissues in the usual way.

Things to Do in the Garden

Gardening is not nearly such a stodgy pastime as many people make it out to be. It all depends, really, on the way that you look at it. Growing plants can be a really interesting occupation. Then there are all the things that come into the garden like butterflies, ants and bees, for instance, which can give you a lot of entertainment if you study them carefully.

The trouble with plants, and particularly growing them from seed, is that some things seem to take so long to grow that you've almost forgotten about them by the time they come up. Or, if you're like me, you find you can't remember what you planted when the first green shoots come up or, even worse, you can remember what it was, but you can't remember *where* you put it, and you spend hours searching the garden to try to find it.

But let's take a look at some things you can do in the garden that show quick results, and at some plants, too, that are curious and interesting to grow. Then there are some tricks you can play with growing things and, most important of all, some nice things to grow that you can eat.

Watch your name growing

Have you got any marrows growing in your garden? If you have, then you can earmark one for yourself by putting your initials on it, and watching them grow too. This is the way you do it: when the marrow is quite small, draw your initials on its side, then take a sharp knife – a penknife is best – and

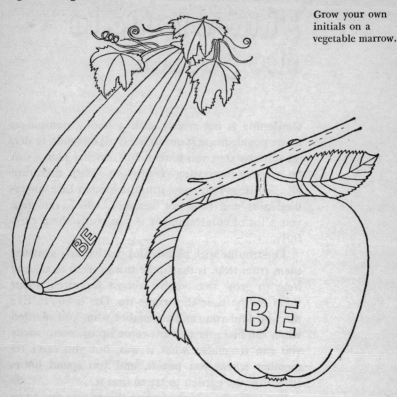

Grow your own initials on a vegetable marrow.

carefully cut out the letters, taking off the skin of the marrow but not digging too deeply into the flesh. Now you can watch your name grow at the same time as the marrow grows, until the letters are really quite a large size – it's a little like the letters on a balloon that is blown up (see sketch above left).

You can earmark plums and apples for yourself, too, in the same way if you want to, especially if the apples are the kind that turn a good, rosy red when they are ripe. This time stick your initials on the side and they stay the same size, of course. Cut the letters out of surgical tape (the kind they use for sticking down bandages) or from the black insulat-

These letters are formed by sticking them, cut out of insulating tape, on to a fully grown green apple; the rest of the apple changes colours but your initials will remain green.

ing tape that your father uses sometimes when he is repairing electrical things. You won't find it very easy to do, for the tape tries to stick to your scissors, but if you are careful not to cut yourself the best way to cut is with the corner of a razor blade. When the fruit is fully grown, but has not yet turned colour, stick the initials in place on the side of the apple or pear or plum that is facing the sun most of the time. The skin under the tape will stay its same greeny-yellowy colour while the rest of the fruit ripens. When it is ready, take off the tape and there are your initials grown on the fruit (see sketch opposite).

Miniature trees

If you've got a lot of patience, and you like caring for plants, you can make your own bonsai tree, which is great fun to do. Bonsai, in Japanese, means 'tray tree' and by that they mean a tree so small that it can grow on a tray. It takes a lot of time to grow – in fact it grows up with you, but the work in looking after it is so small that it's really worth starting one now, then seeing how it develops in years to come. The Japanese are very clever at doing bonsai and this is how they go to work. They take tiny seedlings of oaks or pines, when they have just grown a few inches high, and by trimming the roots and shoots and by training them with wire, they turn into gnarled old trees in miniature. It takes quite a few years to get a really ancient look, but with patience you could have a fairly elderly tree by the time you grew up.

Sycamore and horse chestnut seedlings are the fastest growing ones you can choose for bonsai but conifer seedlings look the best. Search for them on the edge of woodlands, where they often seed themselves among the parent trees. The best ones are those that have been growing for about two years, but it is difficult to tell their age unless you spotted them in the first place in your garden. Having made sure it is all right to do so, dig the seedling carefully out of the ground. Look and see which is the first bud up from the base of the plant – if you're lucky you'll find one about half an inch from the bottom of the stem. Cut the rest of the stem off neatly, just above this bud, now put the seedling in the smallest flower pot that will take its roots, and that's all you have to do to it for two years. Put the pot out of doors in some sheltered place where it will get what rain there is going, but keep an eye on it in the summer time to make sure that it doesn't dry out. In two years' time you cut the stem back again, this time to about one inch high. You allow it to grow for another two years, then cut it back again, this time leaving it a little longer.

By the time you have left school you'll find the seedling will have begun to look a little like a gnarled old tree. If any branches grow, you trim them back into a pyramid shape. Since bonsai take such a long time to grow, it's quite a good idea to grow a family tree, with the eldest child starting it off, and then passing it down to the others, one by one. You keep the tree in the smallest pot you can get away with, because cramping its roots also helps it to age. The Japanese wire the 'trunks' of their miniature trees so that they grow in a twisted way, but I don't like doing that, I think it's cheating.

Ferns from vegetable tops

Now for something that could not be quicker: next time your mother is cleaning some carrot ready for cooking, get her to save the tops that she has cut off. Simply put them, right side up, in a saucer and pour water in until it comes halfway up their sides. Hey presto, within a week you'll have some feathery green, fern-like foliage growing (see sketches

How to grow a
carrot top fern in
a saucer.

above), and you can keep it going for a long time. Carrot ferns look nice growing along the kitchen window-sills in winter (I've got some growing now). You'll notice a funny thing about them – as they grow taller they get top-heavy and you have to weight them down with pebbles to stop them turning over. You can do the same thing with turnips, too, and if you can get a small sweet potato (you can recognize them at the greengrocer's by their pink skin and long sausage-like shape) it will grow something that looks like a vine.

Pineapple plant

If you want to try something really exotic wait until your mother decides to treat you all to a fresh pineapple. Go with her to the shop and pick one that looks young, with nice, healthy-looking leaves. It won't necessarily be the most expensive – the pineapple I grew was from the top of one I bought from Woolworth's – but it needs to look nice and fresh; tired, greyish leaves are no good. When she cuts off the top, take it carefully, dust it with hormone rooting powder, the kind used for geranium cuttings, and put it carefully in a pot filled with peat that has been nicely packed down. The soil should come about half-way up the side of the pineapple, rather like the water up the side of the carrot tops.

Keep your pineapple in a light warm place, water it regularly and, with luck, it will put down little whiskery roots. It's very exciting when you realize that new green leaves are appearing in the centre of the plant, then you know it has 'taken'. If you were exceptionally lucky – and for this you would need a heated greenhouse – you might be able to grow a pineapple to eat. It grows, rather like a hyacinth does, on a central stem in the middle of the plant. But the shiny, rather spiky, leaves alone make an interesting plant.

Gourds and loofahs

What else can you grow that's interesting? Ornamental gourds are easy to raise from packets of seed you can buy anywhere. They grow into all sorts of funny shapes; some are plain, some are striped, some are long, others are bottle-shaped. You start them off in pots early in the year, indoors or in a greenhouse, then in early summer you can put them out in the ground. Once your gourds are fully grown and ripe you pick them, bring them indoors to dry slowly, and then you can cut them open and use them as musical instruments, or simply leave them as they are. If you varnish them afterwards they'll last a long time.

You can grow yourself a loofah for the bath if you want to. Loofahs are grown like cucumbers, in other words on stems that climb and trail. They look rather like cucumbers when they're ripe, too. Where's the loofah? It's in the inside, looking rather like the centre of a marrow.

Insect-eating plant

Now we're moving on to the weirder plants. Some of them prey on things: the Venus fly-trap, for instance, is one of them. You can buy baby ones now in florists' shops (they're imported from Holland, for the Dutch are very good at growing difficult things). The Venus fly-trap looks deceptively innocent, sitting there in its small pot with a plastic dome over it (it has to live under this most of the time to give it the right warm moist conditions, because it is really a tropical plant).

Follow the instructions that come with it, and look after it carefully, and when your Venus fly-trap has grown you'll find that its curious, curved, spiked leaves – I think they look like something from a science fiction film – will close with a snap over any small insect that is silly enough to touch them. But the Venus fly-trap itself isn't all that smart, you can deceive it easily by touching it with a knitting needle. It will imagine then that you are a fly and close up just the same.

Two other oddities

There are two other plants that behave in a very peculiar manner indeed, one that must be grown indoors and another you can grow in the garden. The indoor one is called the semaphore plant (its correct name is *Desmodium gyrans*) and it jerks about in a peculiar manner, just as if it is signalling to someone, if it is left on a hot, sunny window-sill. It's the combination of warmth and light that makes it behave in this way. At night when there is not much of either, it folds itself down just as if it is shutting up shop. The other plant, *Mimosa pudica*, the sensitive plant, can be grown in the garden. It is very delicate-looking, with pretty fern-like leaves, and it has a delicate constitution, too – if you touch its leaves, they close up together, like two hands held together in prayer. Give the *Mimosa pudica* a sharp tap, and often the whole plant will collapse in a heap, poor thing, and take about twenty minutes to recover!

The squirting cucumber

If this is all too sensitive for you, have a go at the artillery plant (its real name is *Pilea muscosa*) which fires off its yellow pollen in puffs of smoke as if it is a gun. Then there's the squirting cucumber (*Ecballium elaterium*) which squirts its seeds at you if you touch it, and sometimes starts squirting of its own accord. Another plant, which you can grow outdoors – it's more of a bush really – is dittany, which gives off a secret gas that you can't see, though if you look very carefully on a hot summer day, and very closely, you may notice that the air immediately surrounding it is affected in the same way as the air over a bonfire – things look wavy and distorted. After a spell of dry weather you can actually set dittany alight without hurting it in any way. Put a match to the bush and it will blaze – but it is only the gas that has caught fire, not the leaves themselves. It's rather like lighting up a Christmas pudding after brandy has been poured over it.

Grow your own jungle

If you're offered a piece of garden to yourself, don't turn it down right away, even if you're not particularly keen on weeding and digging, for a garden doesn't *have* to be a mimsy-whimsy plot with little paths and flower beds, it can be lots of other things as well. You could, for instance, turn it into a jungle to play in if your parents are willing to give you money for some plants. You could put in some clumps of bamboo and of pampas grass and perhaps some giant ferns.

Then there are some interesting grasses like Cloud grass (ask for *Agrostis nebulosa*) and Quaking grass (*Briza maxima*) which shivers all the time. You can also plant some flowers that have interesting seed pods, things like Chinese lanterns with its lantern-like berries; then there is honesty which has large, flat silvery pods. Your mother would like some of these because you can take them indoors in the autumn, dry them off then spray them silver for Christmas decorations.

Things to eat

Grow something to eat – that's another idea. But don't just stick to mustard and cress, or if you do, don't simply plonk it on a piece of flannel in a saucer. Grow it on a potato head or, if you want something that will last longer, mould your own head out of Plasticine with a hollow in the top, and grow it in there – he'll look as though he has a very short crew-cut hairdo.

If you like Chinese food, you can grow your own bean sprouts very easily, just like mustard and cress, and they're easy to cook – you just boil them for a few minutes. Bean sprouts are usually called Mung beans in the seed catalogues, and one packet goes a long way. You grow bean sprouts in the same way as mustard and cress, though it takes a little longer. Don't make the mistake that I did once of sowing too many seeds at once – we had bean sprouts for breakfast, dinner and tea until we'd used them up because I didn't want to waste them!

Square tomatoes

Have fun with fruit – there are all sorts of curious tomatoes you can grow – tiny ones just the size of

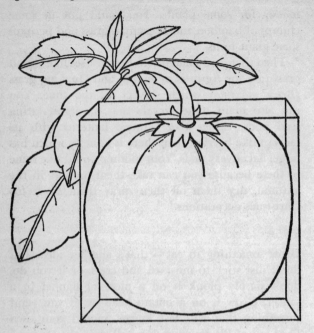

The idea is that the tomato will grow into the corners of the box, so that it ends up cube-shaped.

marbles, that you can pop into your mouth, whole yellow ones, and plum-shaped ones and yellow and red striped ones. You'll find them in most seed catalogues.

I've always been meaning to grow a square tomato, and I can't see why it can't be done – perhaps you'll have a try for me. You need a small, clear cube-shaped plastic box about the size of an ordinary home-grown tomato (I found one with some eye-shadow in it). Slip it over a tomato that is still growing on the plant, choosing the one that fits it the tightest (see sketch above). Now, in theory, the tomato will be unable to go anywhere else and will have to grow into the corners of your cube – that's what *should* happen, at any rate. But let me know if you have a go.

Pear inside a bottle

One thing I *have* done and that you could do, is to
grow a pear in a bottle and, as the advertisements
say, 'Amaze your friends'. You need a bottle with a
reasonably wide neck – a medicine bottle is useless,
a milk bottle doesn't look very good, but there must
be something in between, perhaps with a soft drink
bottle. Find a nice healthy-looking pear on a straight
branch, one that is still quite small, and slip the
bottle over it and fix it in place. Make sure the
bottle is not dragging on the branch, or it might
break off; the bottle may stay in place, held there
by shoots and leaves (as in the sketch below) or
you may have to support it there by twisting wire
round the neck and then round the branch. Now
just leave the pear to grow. If there are a lot of
leaves choking the neck of the bottle, it might be
an idea to take one or two off, so that it doesn't
get all steamy inside, in which case the pear might
rot. It must have light and air.

Growing a pear
inside a bottle.

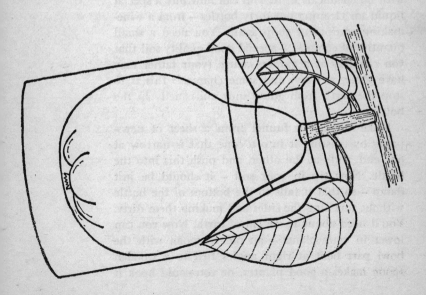

In time you'll find that the pear will almost fill your bottle and it will be impossible, of course, to get it out again. So, just like the mystery ship in a bottle, people will wonder how on earth you did it, when you cut the branch and produce a bottle with a giant pear inside it.

Tiny gardens inside glass

Talking of bottles, growing a garden in a bottle is an interesting thing to do, and it's something that everyone can join in, even if you haven't got a garden of your own. You want a large bottle with a narrow neck – there are big glass ones called carboys, which you see sometimes at garages and you can now buy in shops that sell wine-making equipment. These are very good for big gardens, but there is no reason why you shouldn't take a smaller bottle – a giant pickle one, for instance – and grow a little garden in that. The bottle must be very, very clean and, especially if you got it from a garage, with no chemicals in it. You can now buy a special liquid for cleaning out dirty bottles – from a wine-making equipment shop again. You need a small quantity of compost – special good-quality soil that you can buy at a garden centre (your father may have some, anyway) and some charcoal; this is to stop the earth from going sour and smelly in the bottle.

Make yourself a funnel from a sheet of newspaper by twisting it into a cone that is narrow at one end, wide at the other, and push this into the bottle. Now tip in your soil – it should be just damp – so that it falls to the bottom of the bottle without touching the sides and making them dirty. You'll need about 10–12 cm of earth. Now you can lower in your plants – an old teaspoon with the bowl part bent at right angles tied to a wooden spoon makes a good planter, or you could hook it on a piece of coat-hanger wire. Lower your plants in carefully, and when you have arranged them the way you want them, use a bent piece of coat-hanger wire to brush some earth over them to cover their roots.

If your earth is just moist, then you don't have to do anything more than put a plug of cotton wool in the neck of the bottle, because as the water evaporates from the leaves of the plant and the earth, it will condense on the side of the bottle and run back down again into the soil.

What can you plant in your bottle? African violets do very well, and you can buy those easily in any florist's shop. Wood ferns, mosses and lichens like bottle gardens, too – anything that likes a warm, moist climate and doesn't grow too fast is good for a bottle garden. If this sounds too complicated for you, a disused aquarium can be used as a place to grow plants in in just the same way, provided it has a lid. And you don't have all the bother of doing your gardening with a coat-hanger for you can put your hands straight in.

Looking after your bottle garden

Your bottle garden should not be stood anywhere where it will get too much sun – the glass makes it like a miniature greenhouse and the poor plants would cook if they stood in strong sunlight all day. Try to find a spot that is a happy medium between shade and sunlight and once you've put the garden there, leave it there. Bottle gardens can get rather messy-looking if you keep moving them. You can add little stones, pieces of bark or even plastic toy people, if you want to to liven it up – you could make it look like a miniature jungle if you grew ferns, then put toy tigers and lions among them.

When You're Ill

The most annoying thing about being ill, apart from the fact that you are probably feeling absolutely rotten, is that you're stuck in one place – either flat on your back in bed, or imprisoned in the house because you are spotty, or because you've got a temperature. So the things you can do with your time are limited, rather, to what can be organized on the spot. If you are like me you soon get very bored with simply lying there in bed all day, and even holding up a book to read makes your arms ache. Messy activities like painting and playing with Plasticine are difficult to do, but provided you're careful, a tube of glue can't do much harm, and things done with a pencil and paper and scissors are easy enough to clear away if the doctor turns up unexpectedly. Comics may be soon read and finished with, but it's surprising what you *can* make to play with, even if you have to lie down most of the time.

Sock puppets

Take puppets and stuffed toys, for instance; they're there to keep you company, so you're never alone, and with several you can write yourself a play, and act it out. The simplest puppet to make for anyone who is ill is just converted out of an old sock. Put your hand inside it, pinch the toe end between your thumb and your fingers, and you have a mouth. Stick or sew on pieces of coloured cloth where the eyes and ears should be and you have an animal that looks surprisingly real – if ever you've seen the

American ventriloquist Shari Lewis and her puppet Lamb Chop, you'll know what I mean. If you want to turn your puppet into a bird, you can add a beak made out of two pieces of cloth or paper where your fingers are. And as you have two hands, you can make two sock puppets so they can talk to one another.

Get someone to give you an old cardboard box (a shoe box is fine), knock out the bottom and put your hands up through it, and your puppets look even more realistic, talking to each other behind a 'wall' that hides your arms.

Have you ever tried to do ventriloquism by the way? It's very difficult to describe how to throw your voice but I'll try – though I must admit that I've tried to do it myself, lots of times, without any success at all. You make the words in your mouth in the usual way *but* you don't open your mouth any more than you absolutely must. Try to keep your lips still – move the tip of your tongue instead.

Easy-to-make jigsaws

You can make your own jigsaw puzzles if you've some sharp scissors, cards and a picture from a magazine or Christmas card (see p. 156). You can even make one if you haven't got a picture, but cutting up a sheet of newspaper – fitting the words together – is even harder than fitting the pictures. Don't try and paste your puzzle on to one huge piece of cardboard. It is difficult enough to cut out even if you are sitting up at a table – the cardboard will tend to bend when you cut it in squiggly shapes. Use several pieces of card instead.

Cut up the picture or the newspaper, dividing it up carefully into sections that exactly fit each piece of card, then paste them in place. It makes the puzzle a little easier to do, of course, since you've lots of straight sides to give you guide-lines. But it

Christmas card into jigsaw.

is much easier to handle, lying in bed, and easier to cut out too. Now you draw over the picture or the paper a squiggly jigsaw shape, then cut it out with nail scissors, trying to make the edges as sharp as possible in their outline.

Make-believe stuffed animals

You can make simple stuffed animals in bed by drawing the same shape, of the same size, twice, on to a piece of fabric, then cutting the pieces out and sticking or sewing them together – but remember to leave a hole somewhere to put the paper stuffing in. This kind of animal won't stand up, of course, but then in bed you probably don't want it to. If you are doing this, I think it's much more fun to make fantasy or make-believe animals instead of realistic ones. We made a thing called a Battersea Toot once, out of some black fur fabric I had left over from a coat. No one knows why it was given that name but it had seven legs and both a head and tail at *each* end so it didn't know whether it was coming or going. If you like, you could make a four-humped camel or a four-legged duck or a checked tiger (see below), anything is possible if you are designing it.

Make a life-size doll

You can make a good friend to keep you company quite easily if you're stuck in bed – a really large stuffed toy or doll can be made in a matter of

This cheerful checked tiger is made from a scrap of gingham; his face and tie are felt.

minutes if you can get hold of a supply of old nylon stockings or tights and plenty of newspaper. Simply cut up the tights, stuff them with crumpled-up newspaper and you have arms and legs and a body in no time at all. If you've plenty of materials you could make a life-sized boy or girl using one stocking for each limb – arms or legs – and something wider for the body (you could sew two stuffed stockings together, side by side) or using the body-part of a pair of tights. The head is made in the same way with woollen hair added on and stick-on eyes and mouth from bits of coloured felt.

The simplest doll is made by taking one stocking, first of all. You stuff it, wind some cotton round near one end for the neck (the end piece becomes the head), another where the waist should be. You then stuff another stocking and tie it in a cross form at shoulder level to make both arms, another one folded into an upturned V at the bottom of the body for legs. The advantage of using nylons is that they stretch – you can make your characters long, short or fat or thin. And when you are tired of the whole thing you haven't got lots of cotton wool or other kind of stuffing to get rid of – the newspaper can be simply put into the dustbin and it doesn't make too much mess.

Painted pebbles

Painting pebbles is a not too messy occupation for an invalid if you use felt-tipped pens for the job instead of wet paints. But remember that felt tips will mark the bedclothes dreadfully if you leave them lying around with their tops off and, worst of all, the colour will dry out and you won't be able to use them again. So this is another occasion when it's a good idea to keep everything on a tray where you can see it. The pebbles and stones can be from the seaside or from the garden – get someone to collect them for you, and wash them carefully. Smooth pebbles decorate the best and can be turned into pretty paperweights but sometimes you find oddly shaped stones that look like fish or animals and give you lots of decoration ideas.

The Japanese do some very complicated decorated pebbles which are collected like works of art – and there's no reason why yours shouldn't be thought of in that way too, for it's possible to draw some really pretty patterns on them. You can also stick things on to stones if you have the proper glue (see *Where to Find What*), tiny beads, sequins, pieces of coloured paper, too – in fact by the time you've finished, I'm sure that nobody will realize that it was simply something that came from out of the garden at all.

Decorated boxes and bottles

Another simple and not too messy thing you can do if you're stuck in your bed is to decorate boxes and jars for presents for people, perhaps for Christmas or for a birthday that is on the way. For this you will need some empty bottles or boxes, plenty of brightly coloured wool or string, and some glue. Make sure that the bottle or box that you use is really clean and free from grease first of all, or the glue will not stick to it. With the help of the wool or string you can turn an everyday object like a pickle jar or a round cheese box into a container that people will like to use for something else. If the jar or bottle you have chosen is very large then you should use thicker string to cover it, perhaps even the kind of fine rope that people use for washing lines.

Let's try a jar first. Turn it upside down, carefully spread a layer of glue over the bottom, then coil your string carefully round and round on it, snail fashion, until the bottom of the jar is covered neatly and no glass can be seen. Now turn the jar upright and spread a narrow band of glue up round the side at the bottom and take your string round over this until it too is covered. Then spread some more glue and wind some more string, and so on until you have reached the top.

It's important not to glue the bottle all over before you start or you won't have anything to hold and, anyway, it might dry before you get to it. The more neatly and evenly you wind the string into place, the better your container will look – it's easiest to use a thick kind of cord and quicker too, of course. But it must look right for the bottle – very thick rope would look rather silly on a small bottle and make a clumsy finish. Once the bottle is covered you can decorate it with felt shapes stuck on to the string, or you could sew on tiny sequins and beads to make flower patterns.

You can cover almost anything in the same way – plastic cups, to make pen and pencil beakers, a flowerpot for use indoors. You can also cover boxes with string (it's easiest if they are round ones) but if they have lids remember you must stop your string short, up the sides, where the lid fits, or you won't be able to put it on afterwards. If you are doing this work in bed, it's a good idea to ask for a tray to put the things on; in this way you are less likely to glue yourself to the sheets.

Bottle people

A family of bottle people is fun to make, using the same idea. Glue the bottle all over and wind rug wool round it from base to neck. The head of the doll in our picture is made of a straight length of knitting joined at the sides and pulled over the

Bottle people are
fun to make when
you're stuck in
bed.

bottle neck, and the hair is just plaited wool. Use a
doll's sweater or better still, knit your own, with
two strips for the hands. If you can't knit, you could
just stick on pieces of felt for face, hands and
sweater.

Where to Find What

Chapter 1 *Things to Do in the Country*

The Scout Association have a number of inexpensive booklets on camping, camp-fire cooking, tracking, etc. Get them through your local organization or direct from the Scout Shop, 25 Buckingham Palace Road, London S.W.1.

For key to these tracking signs, see opposite.

Tiny signs and clues, similar to those used by tramps, will tell the hunters which way the trail makers have gone. See opposite.

I HAVE NOT GONE FAR   I HAVE GONE FAR   I HAVE GONE FIVE DAYS JOURNEY

The semaphore message reads: 'My radio is broken.'

Further reading on fossils: *The Wonder of Fossils*, by William H. Matthews (World's Work); *British Fossils* by Duncan Forbes (Black: Young Naturalists' Series); *Fossils in Colour* by J. F. Kirkaldy (Blandford Press); *Tales Told by Fossils* by Carroll Lane Fenton (World's Work).

Chapter 2 *When You're Living in Town*

Special brass-rubbing kits are available in art suppliers' shops, made by Reeves, or you can buy the items separately.

Fabric crayons can be bought from art shops too.

For details about special bus concessions and Rover tickets, contact your local bus station.

Window-sill zoos: For further reading, try to get *Inexpensive Pets* by Joy Spoczynska (Wheaton) or *A Zoo on Your Window Ledge* by the same author (Muller), from your local library.

Livestock dealers are: D. B. Janson, 44 Great Russell Street, London W.C.1; T. Gerrard & Co., Worthing Road, East Preston, near Littlehampton, Sussex; The Tyseley Pet Stores, 771 Warwick Road, Birmingham 11; Alan Robertson, Morison House, South Learmouth Gardens, Edinburgh 4.

Chapter 3 *For Rainy Days*

Carbon paper, Sellotape and typing paper are best bought from an office supplier's if you can; they are usually cheaper there. You can also get photocopies made there or at a stationer's. The same goes for Letraset, etc.

If you can't get large paper bags from a supermarket, try going to an ironmonger, or buying bags that are specially made for keeping rubbish in.

The best wallpaper paste to use is Polycell. You can get it in very small packets and it doesn't stain materials.

Plaster of Paris can be bought at most artists' shops, at some ironmongers and some stationers. You can use Gesso powder instead but it is usually more expensive.

Aerosol sprays for painting monsters can be found in Woolworth's.

Pipe cleaners for making dolls for a doll's house can be bought from any tobacconist for a few pence.

Chapter 4 *Making Music*

The three-chord trick is a useful set of chords you can use on the guitar to accompany yourself for almost any song, especially the folk ones. (Try it for *When the Saints Come Marching In*, to start

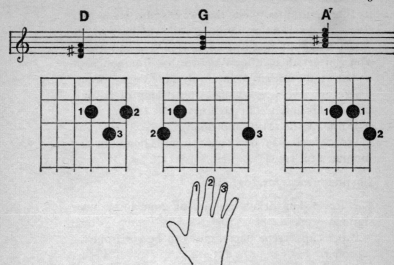

with.) I give them here for both guitar and for the piano.

Chapter 5 *Home-made Magic*

Most toyshops have magician's kits but they are usually rather basic. For more advanced magic, read *John Fisher's Magic Book* (Muller). You'll find others, too, in your local library.

Chapter 6 *Kitchen Cunning*

Good Housekeeping's *Cooking is Fun* is a good book to have around if you want to do some holiday cooking. For quick cheap cream, buy a tin of evaporated milk, boil it for about fifteen minutes *unopened* in a saucepan of water, then chill it until it is thoroughly cold. You'll find then if you turn it out into a bowl you can whip it up to about twice its normal size – it's nice on puddings.

Modelling clay and special wax are among the things you can get from Alec Tiranti Ltd of 72 Charlotte Street, London W.1, who specialize in sculptors' supplies. Modelling wax is also made by Reeves and sold in art shops.

Dylon are the best dyes to use for 'Tie and dye'. You can get them from Woolworth's, ironmongers and the haberdashery counter of many large stores. There are several good books on dyeing of fabric but for 'Tie and dye' in particular read *Tie and Dye* by Anne Maille (Mills and Boon).

Woad seeds can be bought from Thompson & Morgan Ltd, Ipswich.

Chapter 7 *Ideas for Your Party*

For Rover bus tickets inquire at your local bus station.

Paper cups, crêpe paper, etc., can be got from a stationer.

Chapter 8 *Pencil and Paper*

Methuen publish a whole series of books on Origami. Other books worth having on paper folding, etc., are: *Paper Folding and Modelling* by A. van Breda (Puffin); *Children's Costumes in Paper and Card* by Suzy Ives-Ford; *Simple Paper Craft* by Gunvor and Harriet Ask (Batsford); *Paper People* by Michael Grater (Mills and Boon). *80 Things to Make in Cardboard* (Odhams) is another useful book which will give you lots of ideas.

Glue for papier-mâché, etc.: Polycell.

Chapter 9 *On the Move*

For 'Heads, Bodies and Legs' it's a good idea to get a small cheap scribbling pad from a stationers before you go away; it saves tearing up pieces of paper later on.

Chapter 10 *Odds and Ends*

Acrylic paints can be bought at large stationers or artists' supply shops.

The best modelling clay to use if you want something permanent but haven't got a kiln is Das, made in Italy and available at most artists' stores. It dries as hard as a brick and I've never succeeded in breaking it, though I've even put things through a dishwasher and thrown them on to tiled floors on your behalf. Das modelling clay can be painted with anything, preferably Acrylic colour, and you can get bottles of Varni-Das, a clear varnish that makes things shine beautifully after you have painted them, as though they were made from porcelain.

Araldite is a marvellous glue for sticking practically everything together, even china. But it takes a bit of learning to use since you have two tubes and nothing happens until you mix them together – when it happens very quickly.

Special knives and other tools for making lino and potato cuts can be bought at art shops.

Milliners' wire can be bought in some old-fashioned drapers' shops – it's probably easier to get florists' wire from any flower shop.

Araldite is the right glue to use for paperweights, etc.

Chapter 11 *Things to Do in the Garden*

Look out for books on bonsai – there are now several you can get. You can also buy trees that have already been bonsai'd from some garden centres.

Ornamental gourd seeds can be bought from Sutton's, the Venus fly-trap at florists' shops. Bean sprouts come from Sutton's too.

Chapter 12 *When You're Ill*

Old Christmas cards are excellent for cutting up and using as cardboard for puzzles, etc.

Bostik is a good glue to use for decorating bottles, and Araldite for anything more difficult.

We hope you have enjoyed this book.
Some other non-fiction Puffins are
described on the following pages.

How To Survive

Brian Hildreth

Everything you need to know about surviving in a hostile environment – how to build fires and shelters, how to find food and water, vital first aid and herbal remedies, how to read a map and use the International Code of Signals. All these things and many more provide a very useful handbook. Illustrated in black and white by Conrad Bailey.

Paper Folding and Modelling

Aart van Breda

What you can achieve by simply folding a piece of paper is amazing. Animals, boxes, birds that flap their wings, suites of furniture, Christmas decorations, windmills, ships and Viking helmets, are just some of the things you can make if you follow the very clear instructions in this fascinating book, which is essentially for beginners in the art of paper folding.

Making Presents and Other Things

Belinda Price

A cheap, exciting and useful selection of presents and decorations which can be made by anyone with a little patience, glue and a pair of scissors. The step-by-step instructions are easy to follow and are illustrated with diagrams in colour and black and white by Robin Lawrie.

Fun with Collage

Jan Beaney

If you are a collector of pieces of string, nuts and bolts, odd scraps of material, pretty pieces of paper, this is the book for you because it tells you everything you need to know about making beautiful and unusual pictures from the amazing assortment of odds and ends in your home and out of doors.

The Big Book of Puzzles

Michael Holt and Ronald Ridout

A fascinating collection of all kinds of puzzles: riddles to answer, tricks to try out on your friends and family, optical illusions galore, and games to play. Something for everyone in fact, whether you like playing with numbers, thinking up words, working out secret codes, or just puzzling over pictures. Fully illustrated by Peter Edwards.

Something To Do

Septima

Here at last is a book to fill up all the wet days and dull days that produce the question 'What can I do?' in every family. *Something To Do* has suggestions for things children can do at home, indoors and outside, without spending much money or being a terrible nuisance. Each month has a separate chapter so that the games and ideas will fit in with the proper season. February, for instance, has a special section of Things To Do in Bed, and August, the holiday month, has a bunch of ideas to pass the time while travelling. Every month has its own special flower and bird to look for. There are tempting dishes to cook, things to make, games to play, and instructions for keeping pets.

The Puffin Book of Freshwater Fishing

Roger Pierce

This book has been written to introduce the complete beginner to freshwater fishing. It takes him through the early stages of home-made tackle, of learning about the different types of fish and where they are to be found, to the thrills of fly-fishing, spinning and advanced 'fieldcraft'. Illustrated by Michael Shand.

The Pond Book

John Dyson

Nearly all village ponds were man-made and a hundred years ago every village in England had one. This is a fascinating study of how the ponds were made and why, how we can rescue disused ponds and look after them so they remain part of the countryside. There is practical advice on watching the life in and around ponds, building your own aquarium, keeping a field notebook, making a nesting raft and so on. Illustrated in colour and black and white.

The Insects In Your Garden

Harold Oldroyd

How much do you know about the insects that come to your garden or into your house to find food and shelter? What exactly do they do in their short, uncertain lives? We can learn a lot about insects by studying them in their natural world – in the garden, or house, in fields or ponds, in the morning or at night. This book will tell you where to look for insects, and what to watch for, how to catch, mark and care for them. Illustrated in black and white by David Halliwell.

If you have enjoyed reading this book and would like to know about others which we publish, why not join the Puffin Club? You will be sent the club magazine, *Puffin Post,* four times a year and a smart badge and membership book. You will also be able to enter all the competitions. For details of cost and an application form send a stamped addressed envelope to:

The Puffin Club Dept A
Penguin Books Limited
Bath Road
Harmondsworth
Middlesex